*exploring*

# HEAVENLY PLACES

## *TRAVEL GUIDE TO THE WIDTH, LENGTH, DEPTH AND HEIGHT*

### VOLUME 9

*Be strengthened with might through His Spirit in the inner man, that Christ may dwell in your hearts through faith; that you, being rooted and grounded in love, may be able to comprehend with all the saints what is the width and length and depth and height—to know the love of Christ which passes knowledge; that you may be filled with all the fullness of God.*
*Ephesians 3:16a-19*

*exploring*

# HEAVENLY PLACES

## *TRAVEL GUIDE TO THE WIDTH, LENGTH, DEPTH AND HEIGHT*

### VOLUME 9

BY

# Paul L Cox

# Barbara Kain Parker

# EXPLORING HEAVENLY PLACES, VOLUME 9
## *TRAVEL GUIDE TO THE WIDTH, LENGTH, DEPTH AND HEIGHT*

### By Paul L Cox and Barbara Kain Parker

Aslan's Place Publications
9315 Sagebrush Street
Apple Valley, CA 92308
760-810-0990
www.aslansplace.com

Unless otherwise indicated, scriptures are taken from the:
**New King James Version (NKJV)**: New King James Version®. Copyright © 1982 by Thomas Nelson. Used by permission. All rights reserved.

Some scripture quotations are from The ESV® Bible (The Holy Bible, English Standard Version®) copyright © 2001 by Crossway Bible, a publishing ministry of Good News Publishers. Used by permission. All rights reserved.

Copyright 2018, by Paul L Cox and Barbara Kain Parker
All rights reserved.
Editor: Barbara Kain Parker
Cover Design: Brodie Schmidtke
ISBN # 978-1-5136-2592-8
Printed in the United States of America

# TABLE OF CONTENTS

# INTRODUCTION

In the *Exploring Heavenly Places* series, we routinely speak of the places we visit in the spiritual realms, which exist beyond our physical reality and are far removed from the everyday comprehension of most people. We have defined over twenty of these destinations in our *Discernment Encyclopedia for God's Spiritual Creation (Volume 7)*, but have only written more extensively about a few of them (i.e., depth, grid). Now the Lord has impressed upon us that it's time to explain more about our destinations as we travel in His Spirit. Notice that last phrase, "...as we travel in His Spirit". We never, ever, attempt anything that is not Spirit led, following Jesus' example to follow the Holy Spirit and to do only what the Father is doing:

> *Immediately the Spirit drove Him into the wilderness.[1]*

> *Most assuredly, I say to you, the Son can do nothing of Himself, but what He sees the Father do; for whatever He does, the Son also does in like manner.[2]*

Granted, many people do experience and travel into the spiritual realms, following the advice of their favorite self-help yogi or guru to go inside ourselves and hopefully find meaning, wisdom, tranquility, etc., or to locate a spirit guide for direction. Some actively practice astral projection, a technique rooted in esotericism and occultism, in which there is an out of body experience as the soul or consciousness leaves the physical body and travels about the universe,[3] or the grid as we know it.

Rest assured, this is not that! The only 'spirit guide' we heed is the Holy Spirit of the Living God, and as we explore God's modes of transportation and His righteous created places, biblical evidence will be presented that validates our experience.

Fasten your seatbelts as we take off on a journey into areas of the width, length, depth, and height that lie beyond the understanding we had when *Exploring Heavenly Places, Volume 1* was written. It should be an exciting journey, for:

*Eye has not seen, nor ear heard,*
*Nor have entered into the heart of man*
*The things which God has prepared for those who love Him.*[4]

Happy traveling, and stay tuned for future volumes that explore other heavenly places!

Paul L Cox
Barbara Kain Parker

[1] Mark 1:12
[2] John 5:19
[3] https://en.wikipedia.org/wiki/Astral_projection
[4] 1 Corinthians 2:9

CHAPTER ONE

# GOD, OUR TRAVEL AGENT

Online or down the street, travel agencies compete to offer the best deals and lure people in with beautiful pictures of exotic locations. Each one offers package deals, convenience, competitive pricing, and every other lure they can think up to entice customers to fly away to pristine beaches, float down a river in Europe, cruise to Alaska, go on an African safari, or discover just about any other locale known to man. Plus, it's only a matter of time before flights into outer space become routine travel for the everyday individual, with one company already hard at work to complete development of their spaceport in southern New Mexico for public use.[1]

Imagine what sort of catchy ad God could write if He were a travel agent. Perhaps it would look something like this:

---

NOW OFFERING TRAVEL TO EXOTIC LOCATIONS BEYOND TIME & SPACE

*Featuring:*
- *Free travel (all costs pre-paid by a generous donor)*
- *Guaranteed on-time arrivals*
- *Locales never before experienced by mankind*
- *Time and outside-of-time travel*
- *Destinations may be accessed without leaving the comfort of home*

Disclaimer: Must agree to follow travel agent's itinerary.

---

At first glance, God's advertisement would appear to be almost to good to be true, but it's not. He stands ready, willing and able to transport His people into the unseen dimensions that we refer to as the heavenly places. But take heed of the disclaimer! One must be willing to follow His agenda, go only where the Spirit goes, do only what the Father is doing, and be willing to adhere to His perfect timing.

How can this be? We are firmly rooted in a physical realm that is measured by the dimensions of time and space. Or are we? The reality is that we are very multi-dimensional, and as Paul Cox often says, "We are much bigger on the inside than the outside." Biblical proof of that? Yes. First, as Christians we are already seated in the heavenly places:

> But God, who is rich in mercy, because of His great love with which He loved us, even when we were dead in trespasses, made us alive together with Christ (by grace you have been saved), and raised us up together, and made us sit together in the heavenly places in Christ Jesus.[2]

Not only that, but the Spirit of God lives within our bodies, and we cannot even begin to guess how big He is. So how does He fit? Such an unseen reality defies imagination, so we simply accept His word at face value through faith:

> But if the Spirit of Him who raised Jesus from the dead dwells in you, He who raised Christ from the dead will also give life to your mortal bodies through His Spirit who dwells in you.[3]

> Do you not know that you are the temple of God and that the Spirit of God dwells in you?...For the temple of God is holy, which temple you are.[4]

As we consider heavenly travel with God, perhaps it would be good to consider what that looks like. An earthly travel agent would routinely offer various modes of transportation, and whether it's a walking tour of an historic site, a donkey ride to the bottom of the Grand Canyon, bicycling through France, driving, riding, floating or flying; each trip is highly personalized. God's trips are also individualized, with each person discerning what is happening through their five senses according to their spiritual gifting, as well as though Spirit-sent words of knowledge. The Apostles Paul and John were both familiar with such travel, with Paul's experience being so reality-based that he actually didn't know if he experienced it in his body or not:

*I know a man in Christ who fourteen years ago—whether in the body I do not know, or whether out of the body I do not know, God knows—such a one was caught up to the third heaven. And I know such a man—whether in the body or out of the body I do not know, God knows—how he was caught up into Paradise and heard inexpressible words, which it is not lawful for a man to utter.*[5]

On the other hand, John clearly revealed that he was in the Spirit and that his travels were spiritual excursions into heavenly places:

*I was in the Spirit on the Lord's Day, and I heard behind me a loud voice, as of a trumpet...*[6]

*Immediately I was in the Spirit; and behold, a throne set in heaven, and One sat on the throne.*[7]

*So he carried me away in the Spirit into the wilderness.*[8]

*And he carried me away in the Spirit to a great and high mountain, and showed me the great city, the holy Jerusalem, descending out of heaven from God...*[9]

An e-ticket ride in modern-day vernacular indicates a ride that is very exciting or fun, but the term dates back to the 1950s through the 1970s when a visit to Disneyland involved the purchase of a ticket book that included an assortment of tickets designated as A, B, C, D, or E. The E tickets were the best, and it always seemed like there just weren't enough of them; but to use up the whole book and get your money's worth, one would settle for a trip to the King Arthur Carousel (A) or the Swiss Family Treehouse (B), instead of the Matterhorn Bobsleds or It's A Small World (E). The good news for us is not that Disney changed their way of doing things in the 80s to include all-park passes in the price of admission, but that God provides attractions that routinely exceed the satisfaction of an E ticket, and at no cost because Jesus has already paid the full price of admission.

There's no need to settle for less than God's best, so we can eagerly anticipate the thrills that will be ours as we travel in the Spirit to His heavenly places, not only receiving revelatory knowledge and wisdom, but also deliverance. We should never limit our expectations of what He can and will do, for we will experience His presence and power as never before if we allow Him to take us where He will.

First stop, a retrospective look at where we've been…

[1] http://www.virgingalactic.com/spaceport-america/
[2] Ephesians 2:4-6
[3] Romans 8:11
[4] 1 Corinthians 3:16, 17b
[5] 2 Corinthians 12:2-4
[6] Revelation 1:10
[7] Revelation 4:2
[8] Revelation 17:3a
[9] Revelation 21:10

## CHAPTER TWO

# *IN RETROSPECT...*

As the number of books in this series grows, Paul and I face a dilemma: we can often not recall the exact details of what we've already covered, or even which volume a particular discussion is in. In fact, as we talked about the idea of this book taking up where we left off in *Volume* 1, [1] Paul groaned, "I can't even remember what we wrote!" So, this chapter is as much for our benefit as it is for our readers because, as is often said, "You can't know where you're going if you can't remember where you've been."

As often happens, many prophetic words are not understood at the time they are received, and only become clear once we are well into a journey to one of God's revelatory destinations. In this case, it all began in 2006, when a prayer minister first had a dream, and later a vision, about being a minor (only to realize much later the word referred not to a minor child but to a miner). It wasn't until 2008, when two different intercessors delivered prophetic words that began to put things in context that we finally began to understand that this was about the depth. Paul wrote:

> We have been told for a long time that we must go higher; we must go higher; we must go higher. But now the Lord was clearly saying, "You must go deeper; you must go deeper; you must go deeper. You must know the deep things of God which are not in the height, but they are in the depth." We suddenly found ourselves on a new frontier of knowledge. This revelation of the depth has opened new realms for personal healing...The revelation of the depth has been one of the most profound revelations the Lord has given us, as well as one of the most difficult to receive and believe. I remember so clearly when the revelation was coming that I found myself in disbelief that the insights were true. At one point an intercessor was giving a word from the Lord when she turned to me and said, "The Lord says, 'Stop

being so religious and listen to me.'" I was shocked by the comment but opened my spirit and mind to truly listen. So often in this journey I am forced to take a leap of faith, re-examine the Bible, and walk out what the Lord is revealing. That has been difficult. However, as ministry takes place and people's lives are changed, faith turns to true belief.

"People's lives are changed," is such an important aspect of our ministry! We first do what we do out of obedience to the Lord but like everyone else, we long to see the fruit that results, and such fruit exists! Some testimonies of deliverance and healing are included in *Volume 1* and the evidence continues to grow.

By 2009, our understanding of the depth had been refined to the point that we developed the *Prayer to Release One from the Ungodly Depth*, which is a generational prayer seeking deliverance from the places in the ungodly depth that we had identified as Sheol, Hades (Greek)[2], death and fear; as well as the snare, trap, perdition, pit, net, darkest place, utter darkness and deep darkness. Shortly thereafter, with ongoing revelation, the *Prayer to Release the Treasures of Darkness* was added.[3]

These prayers were life changing for many, which was very exciting, but we didn't realize at the time that God was also going to grant understanding of the width, length and height:

> *...may be able to comprehend with all the saints what is the width and length and depth and height...*[4]

This new level of revelation began with Paul and Rob Gross[5] during a ministry trip to Hong Kong in 2011, as they were dining in a restaurant one evening. Both experienced a new discernment and by asking many questions of the Lord, they finished dinner with a new direction but more questions than answers.

Paul's research showed that no one seemed to know what the width, length, depth and height are; with commentators offering only speculation, and pretty-much dismissing those words with explanations that make sense only according to human experience and understanding coming from the purview of our physical reality. He decided to examine the context of verse 18 in light of the surrounding verses (hmmm, what a concept!):

> *For this reason I bow my knees to the Father of our Lord Jesus Christ, from whom the whole family in heaven and earth is named, that He would grant you, according to the riches of His glory, to be strengthened with might through His Spirit in the inner man, that Christ may dwell in your hearts through faith; that you, being rooted and grounded in love, may be able to comprehend with all the saints what is the width and length and depth and height—to know the love of Christ which passes knowledge; that you may be filled with all the fullness of God.[6]*

Paul concluded that the Apostle Paul used several terms that link to the width, length, depth and height. These are: the mysteries of Christ, evangelism, perseverance through trials, strengthening of the inner man, the love of Christ, the working of God's power and unity. He wrote:

> This is the end of what we can intellectually conclude about the width, length, depth, and height; and we are exactly at the place the Lord wants us to be—totally dependent on Him to give understanding and wisdom. We must depend on Him for the revelation of these mysteries. It is now time for the Holy Spirit to reveal the secrets about the width, length, depth, and height.

But that was then and this is now, to use another cliché saying, and now is undoubtedly still just the basic foundation of things yet to be revealed. Nevertheless, keep your seatbelts fastened as we continue our heavenly exploration.

---

[1] *Exploring Heavenly Places, Volume 1* was published in 2014 (3 years ago), and contains a full account of our understanding up to that point. Please reference chapters 11-15 for more information.

[2] When the Hebrew Scriptures were translated into Greek around 200 BC, the word 'Hades' (the Greek underworld) was substituted for Sheol.

https://en.wikipedia.org/wiki/Sheol

[3] Both of these prayers are available in *Exploring Heavenly Places, Volume 1*, or online at http://aslansplace.com/language/en/about-aslans-place/

[4] Ephesians 3:18

[5] Rob Gross is the pastor of Mountain View Community Church in Kaneohe, Hawaii; he is the co-author of *Exploring Heavenly Places, Volume 2: Revealing the sons of God* and the author of *Volume 6: Miracles on the Mountain of the Lord.*

[6] Ephesians 3:14-19

CHAPTER THREE

# *BUT WAIT, THERE'S MORE*

Perhaps you're familiar with captivating voice of the late Paul Harvey, heard for decades over radio and TV. If so, his famous line, "and now you know the rest of the story" at the conclusion of a broadcast is probably very familiar. His captivating tales could keep you on the edge of your seat, eagerly waiting for the conclusion when a key element, often the name of some well-known person, would be revealed.

The Lord has an even more captivating voce than Paul Harvey did, but about the time we think we've heard 'the rest of the story' there's even more. In this case, more about the depths, and in a few years we won't be at all surprised to have learned that the content both in *Volume 1* and this book has only scratched the surface of what God is yet to reveal. Jana Green's[1] prophetic word from November 2, 2009, seems more relevant now than ever:

(We are in the depths; we are going down deeper.)

The sound is in the water; the water carries the sound. To the depths where the treasure is; down, down, down; deeper still. You have not known the depths yet to be revealed; you have just begun to know the treasures. Go for the gold; go for the gold.

Each level has a different understanding, a new revelation, a new expansion. Unveiling of understanding. I am breathing on the elements. It is in the depths that you are bound together.

Unity, unity; connected together in love; surety in the promises from above, height meets depth where things are revealed. It is an unveiling of treasures; it is beyond measure; it is in the heart of love.

There is healing here; there is forgetting of pain; forgetting of wrongs; renewing of minds into hope that is strong. It is the depths of hope that reveals your faith. Faith has substance and this is the place; it is tangible; it is real; it is what always was, and it is HERE.

We are going down again. Discover; learn what life is. It hasn't been for a long time; you will begin to experience it; true wine and dine.

Restoration of hearing; here you learn to listen. You hear the true sound that is not lost. I wash away all negativity; I will cleanse your thoughts. Your neutral pathways are ready to be restored. Transmission has been blocked off but now you are ready to move ahead. Place of sanctuary; place of peace; a level of rest you have just now reached. Place of union, with inexpressible words, the sound is in the water; here you will not be disturbed. No shame, no correction; no time; it is a knitting together in love. It has not been for nothing. This the Lord will prove.

It is a new beginning, and it will take some practice. You can't right the wrongs; you can't count the cost or you will lose the true value and only see what is lost. Here, your perception changes. The sound will bring sight to see yourself in the Lord. It is in the true light. There is a reflection here where you see face to face, the true reflection in the power of grace. It is the depth of His heart. You will see each other as I do. It is the true perception that will bring you through. You can stop here and you can even win, but for the true treasures and wealth, you have just begun. It is the treasures of darkness in the dark places of the depth.

As our journey into the heavenly places continued, one word after another encouraged us to go deeper and deeper still, and it became very clear that going higher was dependent on going deeper, as in the following excerpts of words from Tobias Renken[2] in April 2012:

Higher places being restored; the depths are being opened up to go deeper and higher so we won't miss the appointment of the Lord, His power...The message is coming like flowing water; The Lord's word is like water...The water of the depth; the strength of the deep; the water of the depth given for generations...the Lord is pressing into deeper places. I see an aquifer underneath and in the sky...the aquifer in the firmament. Going deeper to go higher; cloud in the sky; higher in the cloud; He is set above the stars.

Stir the waters of the depth so you can see the stars in the height. You have not risen to the height; you have just started; just the beginning...Ancient heights and higher heights; dig so far; you have just started; there is gold but it is deeper and deeper till the waters flow...

As revelatory words are received, we always test them with scripture as we seek to unravel what they mean, which often takes years. The prophetic words above by Jana and Tobias offer a good illustration since they both spoke of the waters:

> *The fountains of the deep and the windows of the heavens were closed, the rain from the heavens was restrained.[3]*

> *The waters nourished it; the deep made it grow tall, making its rivers flow around the place of its planting, sending forth its streams to all the trees of the field.[4]*

Two-and-a-half years later in October 2014, Tobias related the following message to Paul:

> The depth is not done with yet, Paul. There are deeper places in the depth that you do not know, higher places you have not touched, a new touching... Treasures of the deep you have not seen, though you have seen some... It is hidden, Paul. Do you now see it is hidden? Logic cannot bring you here; revelation can only point you here; it is hidden; you need more; not logic; not revelation; you need more. Trust in Me I am the everlasting God. My

resources are more resourceful. I will guide you higher and deeper and wider and lower... The treasures lie deep, deep, deep in enemy territory. You will walk and you will run in disguise through the depth, the dark and the sky. You will bring down what is high and lift up what if low. For the mountains will be brought low and the valleys lifted high for Jesus... You have started to receive the treasures but they are deep; treasures to be revealed and broken open.

The depths continued to be revealed, and as we moved into 2017, it's interesting to note that the prophetic words began to mention 'depths of (something)'. On January 12th, Jana sent this greeting to Paul:

Happy Birthday Paul,

I AM's Love letter: You are coming into breakthrough like you have never known. Not always a suddenly, but it will be a shuttle for growth. You ventured in where none have gone before, the depths of dimensions in the obedience of the Lord.

Next, on January 15th, Paul discerned an eagle that sits on his shoulder for the first time in many years. He called Larry Pearson, who received a wonderful word about new beginnings and bigger and better things, ending with:

The eagle is here to carry us into the depths of I AM and distribute the depths of His heart.

In the context of a much longer word for a client in February, Jana said:

No weapon formed against you will have its way. For I have made evil to be destroyed. It will certainly have its day. But as for now, you will align your heart within the depths of eternity. That is where you start.

Finally, on June 27th, a message received by Jana from the Spirit of Counsel:

> Oh, the <u>depths of the riches of wisdom and knowledge</u>, unsearchable judgments and unfathomable ways [of God]. How to know the mind of the Lord and who became counselor except the Word that restores? For from Him and to Him are all things in the glory forever, from beginning to end. This is how you believe. (A sensation of going down surrounded by water) Deeper still without a bottom; a restored hope stays in this place...Order upon order, it was aligned to be right. Building on the components of the elements in the womb of the dawn, and then locked together in the <u>depths of the earth</u>, the Father composed you as a song; harmony that brings balance, a chromatic scale; frequency, light and color so the flesh would prevail...

It is abundantly clear that God's righteous depths overflow with treasures for His sons and daughters, and we learn about them through Wisdom, who dwells in the heights:

> *Yet among the mature we do impart wisdom, although it is not a wisdom of this age or of the rulers of this age, who are doomed to pass away. But we impart a secret and hidden wisdom of God, which God decreed before the ages for our glory. None of the rulers of this age understood this, for if they had, they would not have crucified the Lord of glory. But, as it is written, "What no eye has seen, nor ear heard, nor the heart of man imagined, what God has prepared for those who love him"—these things God has revealed to us through the Spirit. For the Spirit searches everything, even the depths of God.[5]*

The stage is set for ongoing depths of revelation, our focus here beginning with the deep and then moving on to the height, width, and length.

[1] Jana Green is a prayer minister and is also the gifted artist who contributed the drawings in *Exploring Heavenly Places, Volume 7: Discernment Encyclopedia for God's Spiritual Creation.* Her website is http://www.signsandwondersstudio.com

[2] Tobais Renken is a long-time friend of Aslan's Place, and a gifted prophetic intercessor. He lives in Germany and is a frequent contributor to the Exploring Heavenly Places webinars.

[3] Genesis 8:11

[4] Ezekiel 31:4

[5] 2 Corinthians 2:6-10

CHAPTER FOUR

# *A PARENTHESIS*

A parenthesis is an interlude or interval that may be inserted into a passage that is otherwise grammatically complete without it;[1] and it seems that a parenthetical chapter integrating our previous understanding with newer revelations of the width, length, depth, and height is wise at this point.

God was speaking about the deep long before we were aware that it is distinct from the depth, though it does seem to exist at the deepest level of the depth. There is also much more understanding now about the other dimensions than when we wrote the first volume of *Exploring Heavenly Places*. In that book, our focus was mostly on the ungodly depths, with a short chapter introducing the *Prayer to Release the Treasures of Darkness*. No sooner was it written than the revelation of other aspects of the depth began expanding, along with increasing insights regarding the width, length and height. We continued on our journey, going deeper in order to go higher.

> *...they saw the deeds of the Lord, his wondrous works in the deep.*[2]
>
> *In his hand are the depths of the earth; the heights of the mountains are his also.*[3]

Though we didn't realize it at the time, the revelatory hints about the significance of the deep began in October 2006, when a participant in a session of discernment training and exploration shared:

> I have put my seal on the ancient pathways. The land is frozen in time as I have purposed it for this time, only I will open the gate to go through. I have sent my teachers, my ancient ones to teach, teach, teach. The ways for the secrets of the deep are very, very precious to my heart. It is a revelation of the days of old. This knowledge has been preserved throughout time. I froze it before the earth was

finished; I have kept it safe, for many have desired its beauty, its riches, and its wealth in the spirit world. [This is] knowledge that was not written in books of earth and only ones that safely guard these rich treasures can know the secrets of my heart. Life existed long, long ago and I have sent my old ones to give gifts to those who are commissioned to do the work. You are to receive the treasure, the books, the papers, the maps; the seal will be broken at the appointed time. I am coming and I want the world to know that life is precious to me; what was then is to be known now. The ancient civilization exists, frozen deep, deep; I have preserved it for it is precious.

> *From whose womb comes the ice? And the frost of heaven, who gives it birth? The waters harden like stone, And the surface of the deep is frozen.*[4]

In January 2008, as part of a longer word, Persis Tiner[5] wrote:

> Open wide your beliefs
> Eyes that see changes
> Eyes that go deep
> Eyes that I need
> Piercing the deep

During a conference in August 2008, an attendee had just shared from Psalm 36 when a lady commented, "There are secrets in the deep," an observation that is biblical:

> *He reveals deep and secret things; He knows what is in the darkness, And light dwells with Him.*[6]

In August 2009, our understanding of the depths had barely begun when Josiah Peterson[7] wrote the following poem. Its prophetic significance cannot be understated, beginning with the peace that is available to us in the depths of God's love and ending with 'exploring the deep':

> I came to the depths and I found peace
> In the place where co-creation finds release

As entered into the deep rest of Love's being
To be known and to know my soul is pleading
For the knowledge of God so deep calls
In the depths love insuppressible overflows the walls
Deep in the place of being filled to overflowing
Loving being intimate with you
Loving and knowing
Deep in His love finding rest
Laying at His feet
Knowing I am blessed
Laying at the Lover's feet
Joy causing me to weep
All my cares begin to fleet
Exploring the deep

During a Joel's Well meeting in August 2009, a participant delivered a word:

> I am about to release the fountains of the deep. It will be both a revelation and an event. There will be signs and wonders on the earth and in the heavens of the revelations of the fountains of the deep. It is opening; cracks in the earth and cracks in the Spirit; fulfillment and re-visioning; the Spirit is crying out will you not go deeper? Many will hear and few will follow; release it, release it, release it; it is within you.

Fast forward to August 2013, when in the context of a longer word from an angel, Rob Gross said:

> Don't be afraid to venture out into the deep. It's a safe place and it's fun. You don't know what fun is until you see what I have in store for you. Who wants to have fun?

Finally, in December 2013, the Angel of the Lord delivered a tongue, and the interpretation was:

> My people have yet to know my justice. The house of their treasury is at hand. The heart has been sick and many have grown cold, but I have sent a new fire from of

old. There is a resurrected hope not yet explored. My judgments are in the great deep and cannot be ignored.

Once again, scripture verifies the word:

*Your righteousness is like the mountains of God; your judgments are like the great deep; man and beast you save, O Lord.*[8]

The message from the Angel of the Lord continued:

Now I show you in a world of injustice, the lightnings of God for abundance. Many will see and will trust, but for those who have been set apart I will unlock what is beneath and above.

You will soon learn what is to know heaven on earth. For you take the gates of injustice from a heart of truth and worth. A greater sound for a listening ear will bring sight for the face of God to appear. I know this, not one will be left behind who desires to know truth from a heart divine.

And so it happened! The New Year of 2014 would prove to be the time when the Lord began unlocking some of His mysteries of the deep.

---

[1] https://www.google.com/search?client=safari&rls=en&q=parentheses+definition&ie=UTF-8&oe=UTF-8

[2] Psalm 107:24

[3] Psalm 95:4

[4] Job 28:29-30

[5] Persis Tiner is a prophetic intercessor, prayer minister and long-time friend of Aslan's Place

[6] Daniel 2:22

[7] Josiah Peterson is a prayer minister, intercessor and long-time friend of Aslan's Place

[8] Psalm 36:8

# CHAPTER FIVE
# *THE DEEP*

In *Exploring Heavenly Places, Volume 7: Discernment Encyclopedia for God's Spiritual Creation*, we identified the deep as both an entity and a place and noted that there seems to be a distinction between the deep and the depth, though the Greek word *bathos* may specify either deepness or depth. In the Old Testament, however, the Hebrew seems to be a bit more specific using two words, *bathos* meaning the bottom or the depth,[1] and *tehom* meaning deep, sea or abyss.[2]

It's pretty easy to understand how the deep can be a place, but an entity? The question is easily resolved by the definition we assigned to 'entity' in *Volume 7,* along with illustrative scriptures: unlike beings that have self-determination, move about, and can process information and act on it, entities are more static and function according to a prescribed purpose. Sometimes they may be used or manipulated by a being; they may respond to a command, as when Jesus spoke to the fig tree;[3] or they may even move or speak, as do elements of creation that declare the glory of God.[4]

> *The mountains saw You and trembled; The overflowing of the water passed by. The deep uttered its voice, And lifted its hands on high.*[5]

As in the rest of creation, there appears to be both an ungodly and godly version of the deep, as well as physical and spiritual versions. It seems to be a place of water spirits, and both righteous and unrighteous beings may be discerned there. God's righteous deep is a wondrous place, but before we go there let's get the matter of the unpleasant, unrighteous deep out of the way.

Paul was praying with a client in October 2014, when he suddenly experienced a dry throat and recalled Psalm 69:3:

> *I am weary with my crying; My throat is dry; My eyes fail while I wait for my God.*

Wondering what was unique about this depth, he realized it was in the deep and was tied both to words spoken against the client and to homosexual oral sex (the client was trying to leave that lifestyle). Several scriptures seemed relevant:

> *Therefore Sheol has enlarged itself, And opened its mouth beyond measure; Their glory and their multitude and their pomp, And he who is jubilant, shall descend into it.*[6]

> *For there is no faithfulness in their mouth; Their inward part is destruction; Their throat is an open tomb; They flatter with their tongue.*[7]

> *They sharpen their tongues like a serpent; The poison of asps is under their lips.*[8]

One year earlier, in October 2013, during a meeting in New England, Paul received a scroll in his mouth and handed it to Amybeth Berner,[9] who discerned:

> Forty days and forty nights you've warred in a new way. The battle increases. The iniquity is great. The time is now. The enemy has tormented and tortured through secret ground that he holds against the generational line. Deep places.

Paul noted that he had been asked to commit to minister for forty days in a specific place, and then discerned a depth. The conversation continued:

> Paul: I think this is the deep.

> Amybeth: I feel a lot of sadness and crying here.

> Paul: There is hopelessness and anxiety here.

> Amybeth: These are places of torture and torment the enemy uses against my people. Reverse the curse. Reverse the oath.

> Paul: Oath is stronger than curse.

Amybeth: Oaths that were taken at Mt. Sinai are deeper still. The roots run deep. The enemy holds the ground, but I hold the truth. Oaths made to other gods, sacrifices made to other gods, idols that were brought into the land; they live in your blood, they live in your flesh, they tie you to the depths. Gods of Canaan. (Paul adds, "that is very strong.") Take down the altars; repent for sacrifice; repent for the unborn...

Paul: We have repented so much for all of this, but there may have been an everlasting curse that has been placed on the unborn.

Amybeth: I feel something very hot in my hands.

Paul: It's strange fire; it's not good.

Participant: When Amybeth said the word 'oaths', I heard the curse from Jezebel after Elijah tried to remove her from the region, a death proclamation over Elijah:

> *So let the gods do to me, and more also, if I do not make your life as the life of one of them by tomorrow about this time.* [10]

In other words, if you are not like my counterfeit priests, then...On his own, Elijah was unable to remove her; he needed a different dispensation of power and authority through the double portion. She was like a gatekeeper for Baal, the sponsor of Baal in the region, so when you mentioned oaths, there was something that had to do with the altars of Baal.

Paul: And Astheroth—Baal, and Ashteroth were the two deities of Jericho. God created male and female, but this is about the fallen sons of God creating their own the male and female counterparts. I think this oath is, "I give the enemy, my unborn children as an everlasting oath." We have never repented for this; this is an ah-ha moment! Molech is still in control over Israel; Israeli female soldiers are allowed three abortions per year in order to continue to serve in the army.

Participant: Jezebel also released a curse over the prophets of God to be like the prophets of Baal; in other words, to be counterfeit priests. There is something we need to do to restore the rod of Aaron and the manna to its place. Aaron perverted his priestly role at Mt. Sinai.

Paul: I think it was an oath rather than a curse. There is more of a hit on 'oath' than on 'curse'. So Lord, what does 'oath' mean?

Paul observed that the Hebrew word for oath is tied to the number 770; he was 70 years old; his grandson, Aaron, was 7 on their shared birthday that year; and the number 7 is tied to an oath.

The participants joined together in the following prayer to break the power of evil through dedications to Molech:

Father, on behalf of my generational line and myself back to before the beginning of time, I repent for all of us who made an everlasting oath in a perpetual curse that forever tied us and our descendants to Molech and the fallen sons of God and consigned us to the ungodly deep. I repent for all altars that were established in my family line that perpetually re-empowered and solidified that oath down through the generations. I renounce the worship that took place on the Sabbath at Mt. Sinai that forever cursed the Sabbath and your holy numbers 7, 70, and multiples of 7 as well as all cycles of 7 in time. Lord, please pull all parts of my generational line and segments of my generational line out of the ungodly deep; please gather all spirit and soul parts, all physical parts, and all parts of the generational DNA and RNA and return them to me and my family line through your blood. By the power of the blood of Jesus, I renounce that oath and the perpetual everlasting curse that came upon my ancestors because of the iniquity that took place at Mt. Sinai.

The scriptures are replete with biblical proof of the horrors of the ungodly depth, and lend credibility to the words above regarding the sadness, hopelessness, anxiety, torture and torment that was initially discerned in this place in the deep:

*Let not the floodwater overflow me, Nor let the deep swallow me up; And let not the pit shut its mouth on me.[11]*

*You have put me in the depths of the pit, in the regions dark and deep.[12]*

*Woe to those who seek deep to hide their counsel far from the Lord, And their works are in the dark; They say, "Who sees us?" and, "Who knows us?"[13]*

*"For thus says the Lord God: When I make you a desolate city, like cities that are not inhabited, when I bring the deep upon you, and great waters cover you,[14]*

*For You cast me into the deep, Into the heart of the seas, And the floods surrounded me; All Your billows and Your waves passed over me...The waters surrounded me, even to my soul; The deep closed around me; Weeds were wrapped around my head.[15]*

Enough of the unrighteous aspects of the deep—let's move on to its wonders, for the blessings of the righteous depth far outweigh the horrors of the other and they are accessible to us:

*By the God of your father who will help you, And by the Almighty who will bless you With blessings of heaven above, Blessings of the deep that lies beneath, Blessings of the breasts and of the womb.[16]*

[1] http://biblehub.com/str/greek/899.htm
[2] http://biblehub.com/hebrew/8415.htm
[3] Mark 11

[4] Psalm 19:1-4

[5] Habakkuk 3:10

[6] Isaiah 5:14

[7] Psalm 5:9

[8] Psalm 140:3

[9] Amybeth Berner, a Christian psychologist with a practice in New England, is a long time friend and intercessor for Aslan's Place.

[10] 1 Kings 19:2

[11] Psalm 69:15

[12] Psalm 88:6

[13] Isaiah 29:15

[14] Ezekiel 26:19

[15] Jonah 2:3,5

[16] Genesis 49:25

CHAPTER SIX

# *MYSTERIES OF THE DEEP*

The volume of prophetic insights we have received over the years is massive, and sorting through all of them for hidden truths from the Lord can be like mining for gold. In fact, a word search of 'deep' in Paul's collection of past revelatory journeys resulted in over 2,400 pages, so retrieving the golden nuggets of truth almost required a pick and shovel in order to separate 'deep' from the many uses of the word in other contexts. The information gleaned is of high value; after all, if the deep is important enough for God to mention it in the second verse of the Bible, it certainly must be important enough for us to scrutinize closely:

> *The earth was without form, and void; and darkness was on the face of the deep. And the Spirit of God was hovering over the face of the waters.*

We are often surprised at how many years in the past God began dropping hints of revelation yet to be unfolded. In regard to the deep, Paul's first recollection when we began to write this book was a word from Persis Tiner in April 2014, so the hints that began in 2006 were unexpected. As it turns out, Persis' word was more of a spark that ignited our current revelation:

> It's under the sea
> It's under the sea
> You are going
> You are going
> And it is with me
> The enemy won't like it
> He'll try to intervene
> But I have you covered
> And I have a plan
> To bring revelation & knowledge
> To uncover new gateways
> To explore rich new spheres
> Of my vastness

Of my treasures
I have hidden 'til now
So fasten your sea belts
Expect lots of fun
As you help to implode
What the enemy has done.

Persis simply recorded the rhyme as the Lord gave it to her without a clue about what it meant, but she was she was penning a truth that is not only biblical but is also scientifically proven. It was reported in February 2007, that scientists scanning the deep interior of the earth discovered a vast water reservoir that is at least the volume of the Artic Ocean beneath eastern Asia. [1] Then in December 2013, Australian scientists at the National Centre for Groundwater Research and Training (NCGRT) and the School of the Environment at Flinders University reported the discovery of huge freshwater reserves preserved in aquifers under the world's oceans. These exist under continental shelves off Australia, China, North America and South Africa.[2] How wonderful it is as, once again, the Bible is shown to be the original source of scientific information! Consider the underground source of much of the water for the worldwide flood:

> *In the six hundredth year of Noah's life, in the second month, the seventeenth day of the month, on that day all the fountains of the great deep were broken up, and the windows of heaven were opened.[3]*

We've seen that the deep exists beneath the ocean floor in the physical, but of course there is also a spiritual reality. There seems to be a distinction between the deep and the depths, with the deep consisting of fresh water, while the depths appear to be salt water.

When Larry and Jacqueline Pearson[4] were hosting Paul for an Exploring Heavenly Realms conference in June 2014, at Niagara on the Lake, Ontario, Canada, the Lord began unraveling some of His mysteries of the deep. We always like to point out that such revelation is inevitably deciphered among groups of believers, as is evident in the following exchange:

Paul (notes that a spiritual being has manifested): Let's see...Oh! We are in the deep. Let's look in Ephesians 3:16-19 to understand the deep:

> ...that He would grant you, according to the riches of His glory, to be strengthened with might through His Spirit in the inner man, that Christ may dwell in your hearts through faith; that you, being rooted and grounded in love, may be able to comprehend with all the saints what is the width and length and depth and height—to know the love of Christ which passes knowledge; that you may be filled with all the fullness of God.

Paul: We are in the deep; it is like a spiritual ocean. This being up front is tied to evangelism; it is apostolic, prophetic evangelism...Lord who is this? He? She? He. And he is really big. Is there a biblical name for this being, Lord? Mimi, come up front and receive the word.

Mimi Lowe[5] delivering the word: Holy! Holy! Holy! Holy! Holy! Holy! Proclaim the word of the Lord! Proclaim the Word of the Lord! This must not be taken lightly! The fear of the Lord! The fear of the Lord! It's very powerful.

Attendee: Is El Shaddai here?

Paul: Yes, I am discerning El Shaddai; yes, I am discerning the many breasted one.

Attendee: I hear, "Luminosity".

Paul: Yes, that is strong.

Attendee: Job 28 talks of wisdom; verse 28 says, *"The fear of the Lord, that is wisdom, and to depart from evil is understanding."*

Paul: Yes, wisdom is very strong. (Paul reading excerpts from Job 28), *"Going as deep as man can go...no other man has ever walked here, no lion's paw has ever stepped here...men know how to mine flinty rocks...they don't know how to find wisdom and understanding...it can't be bought...wisdom is far more valuable than gold and glass."*

Paul: Actually, I can hear the sound now.

Attendee: I hear "deep calls to deep".

Paul: Yes...oh, there are dimensions in the deep...there is a sphere of the dimensions in the deep.

Attendee: I saw a giant army with a wave passing through at its head...there was a huge wave and the army was marching through it.

Paul: Oh! This is a tidal wave coming up from the deep, not the ocean! Oh, the spiritual being is very excited about this!

Attendee: Does it have something to do with the great cloud of witnesses?

Paul: I think so.

Attendee: Could one of the beings be inside the other?

Larry: Is he here to unlock something inside the wave?

Attendee: Ancient...

Paul: Yes, it is ancient.

Larry: Is it an ancient attendant of the Ancient of Days to release the wave?

Paul: Yes.

Larry giving prophetic word: This is that from the seven thunders. We will not be able to ride the new waves with the old surfboards if we are stuck in yesteryear. This ancient wave and ancient day will carry new heights and new communications that will have global impact and will awaken a new breed of warriors. It will awaken an organic remnant that will meet together in the air. Build the clouds with praise and we will meet one another in the air; as you build we will come. Build with praise and you will meet together in a new airship; there's an airship where you will meet together in high praise because you are no longer mere earthlings.

As Paul was reading the excerpts about wisdom, the deep had not yet been mentioned in the dialogue, so it is interesting to note that Wisdom declares in Proverbs 8:22-31:

> *The Lord possessed me at the beginning of His way,*
> *Before His works of old.*
> *I have been established from everlasting,*
> *From the beginning, before there was ever an earth.*
> *When there were no depths I was brought forth,*
> *When there were no fountains abounding with water.*
> *Before the mountains were settled,*
> *Before the hills, I was brought forth;*
> *While as yet He had not made the earth or the fields,*
> *Or the primal dust of the world.*
> *When He prepared the heavens, I was there,*
> *When He drew a circle on the face of the deep,*
> *When He established the clouds above,*
> *When He strengthened the fountains of the deep,*
> *When He assigned to the sea its limit,*
> *So that the waters would not transgress His command,*
> *When He marked out the foundations of the earth,*
> *Then I was beside Him as a master craftsman;*
> *And I was daily His delight,*
> *Rejoicing always before Him,*
> *Rejoicing in His inhabited world,*
> *And my delight was with the sons of men.*

The unfolding revelation continued, and in July 2014, Jana Green delivered the following word:

This is a message from Holiness in the deep, which seems to be a place in the lowest depth: "It is like a treasure hunt. This is where you find; this is where you realign. You are not in the wrong place but you are inhibited; you are misaligned but this is the place where you are redefined. It is at the deepest level. This is where you were created in secret. For this is the original design, to be recreated. What was finished at the cross takes you back to before you were lost; the original sound will heal; the new creation is what is hidden in Christ before the foundation of the world before the DNA was disturbed. It was a written program to distort the truth, but this is where you find out the treasures in heaven on earth. This is for the soul; the spirit knows, but the elements testify the truth."

Jana's sense was that the word was tied to the truth of Psalm 139:15-16:

*My frame was not hidden from you, when I was being made in secret, intricately woven in the depths of the earth. Your eyes saw my unformed substance; in your book were written, every one of them, the days that were formed for me, when as yet there was none of them.*

In an email to Paul on September 4, 2014, Jana wrote:

I sense authorities coming and going; revelation is building and growing; a position of women who are yet to stand; a platform of justice to heal the land; Hope established by favor in a broad space; the lines of inheritance have fallen in this place. They will know who they are, led out by the Star; power of grace to align to see His face; no longer victims that just survive; calamity to be broken by resurrection life. Harmony will be a unified key, a sound to unlock the realm and set the captives free. Don't go here and don't go there; go into the deep, a place unaware and follow the Lord through the gate. Justice to turn back the battle by strength, believing is the place where you start. Senses will be enlightened to testify of the heart. Light begets light, and understanding and wisdom will be found in the height.

The following year in May 2015, on the web with Aslan's Place, London, Paul realized they had been taken to the deep and he felt healing. A gate was discerned and he felt a vibration and heard a sound. A key was received, the gate was opened and the vibration stopped. The vibration was a manifestation of a being called Holiness, a water being/spirit that seemed to be in the deep. The key was called Grace. Paul Knight[6] heard a sound that would realign them so they prayed, asking to be realigned, and Paul Cox could discern Majesty. As the discussion continued it was determined that Holiness realigns us, and also has to do with evangelism. Additionally, the river of God and trees of healing appeared to be located in the deep.

[1] https://www.livescience.com/1312-huge-ocean-discovered-earth.html

[2] https://newatlas.com/freshwater-reserves-under-sea/30072/

[3] Genesis 7:11

[4] Larry and Jacqueline Pearson of Lion Sword Solutions are long-time friends and intercessors for Aslan's Place; Larry is a prophet and life coach, and Jacqueline is a musician

[5] Mimi Lowe is a prayer minister and prophetic intercessor. She is also the author of her inspiring autobiography, But God…

[6] Paul Knight is a gifted musician/composer, a prayer minister, and was the leader of Aslan's Place, London, which has now disbanded

# CHAPTER SEVEN

# *GOD AND THE DEEP*

On June 2, 2015, in Plovdiv, Bulgaria a rainbow angel manifested and opened up a well of lava, after which a deliverance from the deep ensued. Then, on June 24, 2015, Tobias Renken heard:

> There is another level. It is like a machine; under water, like a well; but it is not time yet. You are the doctor, Dr. Cox. It is not time yet to understand the depth in the depth—the deep. It is beyond imagination. You do not understand it yet. Time will tell you what this is about. There is a shift to a deeper place, breaking thorough something but not time to understand the deep place. You will know in time, Dr. Cox. You will understand. Who is there to enlarge your place, Dr. Cox? Try to understand who enlarges your depth. Where is the enlargement? Where is the place? The north, south, east or west? Or is it a deeper place in your heart? In your heart, there is a reason why you are not there yet. Search your heart to be prepared. Search your heart with surgery. Search your heart for deeper places yet to come.

> In the deeper place there will be no more pulling. Standing in the place of temptation you will be strong. No more pulling even in destruction. This is the place you find rest. This is where My people find rest because I am strong in the midst of them. I am the warrior, a hiding place free from temptation, the resting place.

> This place has different layers. Maturing will take place. There will come a new seeking. There will come a deeper depth of scripture we have not understood yet; deeper yet; deep truth; no mysticism true enlightenment of the eyes and heart. Desire the truth in scripture as never before in a depth that can't be seen by man; it has to come from Me. Desire the enlightenment of your heart so you may see the deep and the steep.

Deeper places in the heart, deep places of rest, no more striving, deeper truth—sounds good, but can such wonderful concepts be verified? Zophar was quite skeptical as he chastised Job:

> *Can you search out the deep things of God? Can you find out the limits of the Almighty? They are higher than heaven— what can you do? Deeper than Sheol— what can you know?* [1]

Even Solomon, recognized as the wisest man who ever lived, questioned the limits of his own understanding and asked:

> *As for that which is far off and exceedingly deep, Who can find it out?* [2]

Fortunately for us, the Holy Spirit has come to teach us all things, as Jesus promised, [3] and we definitely can search out and understand the deep mysteries of God; the wonders of His deep places can be scripturally verified:

> *But God has revealed them to us through His Spirit. For the Spirit searches all things, yes, the deep things of God.*

What are the deep things of God? Much of what we've already written qualifies; but even more, they are all about Him, as in a portion of another rhyme from Persis in October 2016:

It's not what you think
It's not what you think
It's all about Me
It's all about Me
The lights and the bling
Attracting all things
All are a distraction
From what I want to bring…
…Go deep; go deep
For the pathway of righteousness is waiting to be
Dug up by someone
And blown on by Me

As the heavens proclaim the glory of God,[4] the deeps proclaim His mysteries, His might, His power, His expansive knowledge and wisdom, His presence:

*He gathers the waters of the sea together as a heap; He lays up the deep in storehouses.[5]*

*When the waters saw you, O God, when the waters saw you, they were afraid; indeed, the deep trembled.[6]*

*O Lord, how great are Your works! Your thoughts are very deep.[7]*

*They see the works of the Lord, And His wonders in the deep.[8]*

*Whatever the Lord pleases He does, In heaven and in earth, In the seas and in all deep places.[9]*

*Where can I go from Your Spirit? Or where can I flee from Your presence? If I ascend into heaven, You are there; If I make my bed in hell, behold, You are there. If I take the wings of the morning, And dwell in the uttermost parts of the sea, Even there Your hand shall lead me, And Your right hand shall hold me.[10]*

Indeed, the deep is all about Him!

[1] Job 11:7-8
[2] Ecclesiastes 7:24
[3] John 14:26
[4] Psalm 19:1
[5] Psalm 33:7
[6] Psalm 77:16
[7] Psalm 92:5
[8] Psalm 107:24
[9] Psalm 135:6
[10] Psalm 139:7-10

CHAPTER EIGHT

# *DEEP CALLS TO DEEP*

'Deep calls to deep,' is an often-used phrase from Psalm 42 that is interpreted in multiple ways by different people. Since surrounding context is always important in biblical interpretation, that would seem to be a good place to begin unraveling this amazing statement that is both puzzling and amazing.

King David was in a place of extreme anguish when he wrote Psalm 42, crying out:

> *As the deer pants for the water brooks, So pants my soul for You, O God. My soul thirsts for God, for the living God.*

> *Why are you cast down, O my soul? And why are you disquieted within me? Hope in God, for I shall yet praise Him, For the help of His countenance. And why are you disquieted within me? O my God, my soul is cast down within me; Therefore I will remember You from the land of the Jordan, And from the heights of Hermon, From the Hill Mizar. Deep calls unto deep at the noise of Your waterfalls; All Your waves and billows have gone over me.[1]*

An online search of 'deep calls to deep meaning' offers about 6,930,000 possibilities, and without leaving the first page it quickly becomes obvious that there are three prevailing themes among the listed commentaries and personal blogs:

- David was speaking of one affliction after another overwhelming him relentlessly, as being pounded by a storm; and some indicate that these are afflictions sent by God, as indicated by the words 'Your waterfalls' and 'Your waves'

- David was simply writing what he was seeing and he must have been near a rapidly flowing river or waterfall and was describing poetically the power of the water

- It's about intimacy with God and refers to the deep things of God calling out to the deep things of mankind, a communion of Spirit-to-spirit fellowship

It's interesting to note that the first two concepts are relegated to discerning the physical reality alone, and only the third embraces the invisible spiritual reality. Perhaps we would do well to remember that there are many layers to scripture, as is obvious when we read a well-known verse or passage and suddenly see something new. Perhaps one's perspective as to the meaning of this phrase depends largely on whether or not there is any understanding of the dimensional aspects of God's creation.

Charles Spurgeon wrote:

> In the grandeur of nature there are amazing harmonies. When the storm agitates the ocean below, the heavens above hear the tumult, and answer to the clamor; down comes a deluge of sonorous hail or swift-descending rain, attended with peals of thunder, and flashes of flame. Frequently the waterspout, of which David speaks in the next sentence, evidences the sympathy of the two great waters above, and beneath the firmament; the great deep above stretches out its hands to the great deep below, and in voice of thunder their old relationship is recognized; it is almost as if the twin seas remembered how once they lay together in the same cradle of confusion till the decree of the eternal appointed each his bounds and place. "Deep calls unto deep"—one splendor of Creation holds fellowship with another...

> ...But now, no longer confining so grand a thought to the mere manner in which David employed it, namely, to the double trouble of many of God's saints when two seas meet, and when internal and external sorrows combine, I purpose to use the general principle in other directions, and to show that everywhere where there is one deep, it calls to another, and that especially in the moral and spiritual world every vast and sublime truth has its

correspondent, which, like another deep, calls to it responsively. [2]

It's clear that aspects of both God and man are very deep, so it's a given that 'deep calls to deep' is applicable in Spirit to spirit communication:

> *Oh, the depth of the riches both of the wisdom and knowledge of God! How unsearchable are His judgments and His ways past finding out!* [3]

> *They search out injustice, saying, "We have accomplished a diligent search." For the inward mind and heart of a man are deep.* [4]

Looking again at the context of 'deep calls to deep' in Psalm 42, it seems possible that David could have been trapped in a place of tremendous anguish, an ungodly deep, as he cried out to the Lord. If so, his words could have reflected God's voice calling to him from the righteous deep, just as He does today when we are trapped in such hopeless places.

Regardless of how one interprets the phrase, there is no question that:

> *In His hand are the deep places of the earth; The heights of the hills are His also.* [5]

[1] Psalm 42:1-2, 5-7

[2] http://www.spurgeongems.org/vols13-15/chs865.pdf

[3] Romans 11:33

[4] Psalm 64:6

[5] Psalm 95:4

## CHAPTER NINE
# *INTRODUCTION TO THE HEIGHT*

Mountains; how I love the mountains! And I'm not alone; any season of the year will find many heading there to relax. From mountain climbing or biking, to snow skiing or sledding; from swimming in a mountain lake to skating on its ice; from gathering around a campfire on a warm summer night, to relaxing in front of a roaring fireplace on a snowy winter night, the mountains are an amazing retreat. Flower-carpeted hillsides in the spring or snow-capped peaks in the winter, they are things of such majestic beauty and grandeur that any description seems inadequate.

Mountains are the earthly manifestation of the heavenly heights, so is it any wonder that many significant biblical events happened there? God directed Abraham to a mountain in the land of Moriah to build an alter on which to sacrifice his son, Isaac,[1] likely the same Mt Moriah that became the temple mount.[2] Moses first encountered God at Horeb, the mountain of God,[3] and later saw the glory of God and received His laws on Mt Sinai,[4] a terrifying place because God was there:

> *Then it came to pass on the third day, in the morning, that there were thunderings and lightnings, and a thick cloud on the mountain; and the sound of the trumpet was very loud, so that all the people who were in the camp trembled... Now Mount Sinai was completely in smoke, because the Lord descended upon it in fire. Its smoke ascended like the smoke of a furnace, and the whole mountain quaked greatly... Then the Lord came down upon Mount Sinai, on the top of the mountain. And the Lord called Moses to the top of the mountain, and Moses went up.[5]*

> *The sight of the glory of the Lord was like a consuming fire on the top of the mountain in the eyes of the children of Israel.[6]*

Moving on to the New Testament, it was no accident that Jesus was transfigured before Peter, James and John, and met with Moses and Elijah on a mountain height.[7]

46

The importance of the mountains or high places is a recurring scriptural theme, so it should not be surprising that the enemy has tried from ancient times to establish pagan worship there:

> *For they provoked him to anger with their high places; they moved him to jealousy with their idols.*[8]

Such places of sacrifice were a major contributing factor to the downfall of Israel, as is well illustrated by the encounter of Elijah with King Ahab on Mt Carmel.[9] It should also come as no surprise that Satan sought to increase his authority by taking Jesus to the top of a very high mountain to tempt him in the desert.[10] But we can rest assured that the Most High God will forever reign supreme, far above all of creation on both the physical and spiritual heights, as has been prophesied repeatedly:

> *He who dwells in the secret place of the Most High Shall abide under the shadow of the Almighty…Because you have made the Lord your dwelling place—the Most High, who is my refuge…*[11]

> *Now it shall come to pass in the latter days That the mountain of the Lord's house Shall be established on the top of the mountains, And shall be exalted above the hills; And all nations shall flow to it. Many people shall come and say, "Come, and let us go up to the mountain of the Lord, To the house of the God of Jacob; He will teach us His ways, And we shall walk in His paths." For out of Zion shall go forth the law, And the word of the Lord from Jerusalem.*[12]

> *For thus says the High and Lofty One Who inhabits eternity, whose name is Holy: "I dwell in the high and holy place, With him who has a contrite and humble spirit, To revive the spirit of the humble, And to revive the heart of the contrite ones…*[13]

> *Therefore they shall come and sing in the height of Zion, Streaming to the goodness of the Lord—For wheat and new wine and oil, For the young of the flock and the herd; Their souls shall be like a well-watered garden, And they shall sorrow no more at all.*[14]

*For behold, he who forms the mountains and creates the wind, and declares to man what is his thought, who makes the morning darkness, and treads on the heights of the earth—the Lord, the God of hosts, is his name!* [15]

*And he carried me away in the Spirit to a great and high mountain, and showed me the great city, the holy Jerusalem, descending out of heaven from God...* [16]

The obvious importance of the physical mountain heights reflects the significance of the spiritual heights. That God Himself dwells in the righteous heights is a truth that was well understood by the ancient peoples, as is written in Job, likely the oldest book in the Bible:

*Is not God in the height of heaven? And see the highest stars, how lofty they are!* [17]

*For He looked down from the height of His sanctuary; From heaven the Lord viewed the earth...* [18]

The importance of the heights has always been abundantly clear to the enemy as well:

*"How you are fallen from heaven, O Day Star, son of Dawn! How you are cut down to the ground, you who laid the nations low! You said in your heart, 'I will ascend to heaven; above the stars of God I will set my throne on high; I will sit on the mount of assembly in the far reaches of the north; I will ascend above the heights of the clouds; I will make myself like the Most High.' But you are brought down to Sheol, to the far reaches of the pit. Those who see you will stare at you and ponder over you: 'Is this the man who made the earth tremble, who shook kingdoms, who made the world like a desert and overthrew its cities, who did not let his prisoners go home?'"*

Surely there could be no greater evil than to attempt to ascend above the heights and become like the Most High God! The consequences to Satan and all of his followers are dire, for there is

One who dwells in the heights of heaven, seated at the right hand of the Father; and His name and authority reigns supreme:

> *...Christ when he raised him from the dead and seated him at his right hand in the heavenly places, far above all rule and authority and power and dominion, and above every name that is named, not only in this age but also in the one to come. And he put all things under his feet and gave him as head over all things to the church, which is his body, the fullness of him who fills all in all.*[19]

> *Therefore God also has highly exalted Him and given Him the name which is above every name, that at the name of Jesus every knee should bow, of those in heaven, and of those on earth, and of those under the earth, and that every tongue should confess that Jesus Christ is Lord, to the glory of God the Father.*[20]

Knowing God's eternal truth about His righteous height, we can join with all of creation in the heights of praise:

> *Praise the Lord!*
> *Praise the Lord from the heavens;*
> *Praise Him in the heights!*
> *Praise Him, all His angels;*
> *Praise Him, all His hosts!*
> *Praise Him, sun and moon;*
> *Praise Him, all you stars of light!*
> *Praise Him, you heavens of heavens,*
> *And you waters above the heavens!*
> *Let them praise the name of the Lord,*
> *For He commanded and they were created.*
> *He also established them forever and ever;*
> *He made a decree which shall not pass away.*[21]

[1] Genesis 22:2

[2] 2 Chronicles 3:1

[3] Exodus 3:1

[4] Genesis 34

[5] Exodus 19:16, 18, 20

[6] Exodus 24:17

[7] Matthew 17, Mark 9

[8] Psalm 78:58

[9] 1 Kings 18

[10] Matthew 4

[11] Psalm 91:1, 9 ESV

[12] Isaiah 2:2-3

[13] Isaiah 57:15

[14] Jeremiah 31:12

[15] Amos 4:13

[16] Revelation 21:10

[17] Job 22:12

[18] Psalm 102:19

[19] Ephesians 1:20-23

[20] Philippians 2:9-11

[21] Psalm 148:1-6

CHAPTER TEN

# *EXPLORING THE HEIGHT*

As early as 2006, we have records of prophetic words that God would be taking us higher, and we wrote briefly of what we knew about the height at the time in *Volume 1*, so let's review:

Paul was doing ministry May 2010, when an angel came with a message, and the unexpected happened:

> This is a spiritual being called 'the height'. You must go down to go up. As it was said from glory to glory, the revelation unfolds. Since you have been faithful with the little, I will give you the more. Your fulfillment is in hope. Your desire emanates in delight. Desire makes the way; it opens the way because it is connected to faith—hope, desire, and faith. The seven [spirits of God] all hold the key for the next level to be received. Learn well from this journey; it is a new journey; I will multiply it.

> In this place you take dominion; each level is a position received; each level is a position redeemed, dethroned, and enthroned. Perception is changed. You will learn true ruling, true reigning:

> Every level carries manifold wisdom; wisdom is justified by her children. There is a multiplication of endowment of wisdom at every level; she has hewn out her seven pillars. If the Lord does not build the house, they labor in vain. It is more expansive than compartmentalized; you take dominion on each level. At every door and every gate, wisdom cries out. Every pathway, where the paths meet, you create a path, a new one; you take position by decision, by declaration, by agreement. Every level will hold the decision and an edict will be set; it is the new law for every level by the order of Melchizedek. At one hand the old is done away with; at one hand the new law comes; at one hand the old covenant is done away with; at

the other hand a new covenant. Every time something is agreed upon it is written down and decreed. A level dispensation follows. There is more to come, but not for now, until you reach the 8.

We were familiar with the mention of width, length, depth, and height in Ephesians 3:18, but many questions remained. The angel's message made it clear that the height is a place of dominion, of ruling and reigning, but what did that mean? And what did 'until you reach the 8' mean?

Once we receive new understanding of a subject, it is invariably interesting to go back and look at all of the revelatory pieces we already had but were unaware of, so at this point we need to backtrack to include some words that definitely play into our current understanding. Could it be that Larry Pearson's word almost a year earlier on June 20, 2009, was a foreshadowing of 'until you reach the 8'?

> We are emerging for a converging. I see a mountain coming forth out of the earth; creation groans for the manifestation of the mountain of the Lord; there's a new mountain emerging. You will mount up on a new mountain that I am creating. It's not like the others, not like any you have been on before, for I am doing a new thing.
>
> Re-firing, I'm re-firing with a new fire. New heights; this is the 8th mountain; it's the mountain of God. Concentrate; you've come to Mt. Zion; there is a merging and converging of Mt. Zion.
>
> I've never seen a mountain converging before; the 8th mountain is the mountain of God, something so huge. Governmental mountain, the government of God, everything must submit to the mountain of the Lord…we will be dwellers of the mountain of the Lord.

In January 2010, a participant in an exploration session with no knowledge of Larry's word regarding governmental authority in the heights, prophesied:

> You have only thought you had eyes to see with, and now I give you eyes to see higher and higher; and now you will see in heights what you have never seen before. Revelations in abundance and a new tongue to proclaim the new mysteries of the Kingdom; movers, shapers, ambassadors, government, establishers of the government of God on the earth; man's government toppled and God's government coming in its place. Diplomatic immunity; as ambassador you have been given diplomatic government to establish God's government in place of man's failed government. Lawyers, you will plead the case of many in the courts of heaven and win. I see the gavel coming down and a proclamation of 'not guilty'…

Also in January 2010:

> Jana Green: Come and eat, come and drink. Search for gold. Ask for treasure; there is wisdom untold. Greater understanding for height…New weapons I give to you, new tools I am putting into your tool belt…The people shall come, you will see it, you will see it.

> Rob Gross: In the depths there are new secrets. In the heights there will be new breakthroughs.

As time progressed, the Lord continued to tell us that He would take us to new heights and many prophetic words were delivered, a few of which are presented here.

> Larry Pearson, October 2011:
> The first thing I heard is that it's watershed moment. [It's] preparation of a people to ride into new heights and new dimensions to open up a hidden gate; the mountain of the Lord to be unveiled, a preparation of a people to dwell among the mountain of rest to know my best, to hear and to know, to know and to hear…These will be the

blueprints to go into new heights and new depths of the sea of My love...

Aslan's Place Intercessor, June 2013:
...Through this I will show you new measures of my love, and I will take you to new heights and places in the universe that are yet to be discovered...You'll become proficient in this travel and others will marvel when they see you in places that they have not seen you before...the day is coming; the time is almost here.

Larry Pearson, July 2013:
And it will be smooth sailing, as you understand who you are, where you are, and where you are going. I will carry you into new heights; for shackles are coming off of your steps that have kept you earthbound. I am releasing a flood of light to the eyes of understanding on whoever is toward me, turned toward me.

Multiple participants, August 20, 2013:
Wisdom is here; seven pillars of God; seven pillars of wisdom; seven is perfection. You might think this is all you need. Begin with wisdom and then all else will fall into place. Wisdom. My wisdom is tantamount to every aspect. If you do not have wisdom, what do you have? Turmoil, discord, no harmony. The world out there has lost it's wisdom. Where did the wisdom go? The world lacks wisdom. You, My bride, have wisdom; use my wisdom; it has always been there, but the world has its own wisdom.

Pull down the sound; it is all around; the sound that will cleanse; the sound that will bend; the sound to purify the gate; there is no time to wait; let the sound surround. You have looked and you have looked, and now you have found the sound. Here on the height the sound is right.

Wisdom is a counsel...safety dwells in the council of wisdom. The sound of wisdom breeds a sound mind.

There is a sound coming down to the ground profound; the sound of the profound, coming down; shake the ground, changing the ground on which we walk. There is an opening of new paths that wisdom will lead you into. The sound will clean out vision; the sound will clean out the height. To soar into the height, hear the sound of wisdom.

There is a bigger dimension opening up, uncharted ground and dimension. Wisdom has been sent to take you into the new. Walk circumspectly with wisdom at your side; you will gain a stronger stride. This is where you embrace and are embraced by the Son's light...This being is 'the height'.

As always, prophetic words are subject to biblical truth, and clearly each of the words in this chapter align closely with the scriptures presented in the previous one. Additionally, it's clear in scripture that Wisdom dwells in the righteous heights and Folly, or foolishness, in the unrighteous heights—what a contrast!

*Does not wisdom call? Does not understanding raise her voice? On the heights beside the way, at the crossroads she takes her stand; beside the gates in front of the town, at the entrance of the portals she cries aloud: "To you, O men, I call, and my cry is to the children of man...Wisdom has built her house; she has hewn her seven pillars. She has slaughtered her beasts; she has mixed her wine; she has also set her table. She has sent out her young women to call from the highest places in the town...*[1]

*The woman Folly is loud; she is seductive and knows nothing. She sits at the door of her house; she takes a seat on the highest places of the town, calling to those who pass by, who are going straight on their way, "Whoever is simple, let him turn in here!" And to him who lacks sense she says, "Stolen water is sweet, and bread eaten in secret is pleasant." But he does not know that the dead are there, that her guests are in the depths of Sheol.*[2]

In the heights, we are to rule and reign with Christ (see prayer in Appendix 3), exercising the authority we have through Jesus to govern as the Spirit leads, to travel into new heights of revelatory experience with Him, to experience wisdom, understanding, revelation, instruction, and breakthrough.

> *The fear of the Lord is the beginning of wisdom, And the knowledge of the Holy One is understanding.*[3]

Yes, wisdom has built her house in the height, and this is where we ought to live.

[1] Proverbs 8:1-4, 9:1-3 ESV

[2] Proverbs 9:13-18 ESV

[3] Proverbs 9:10

## CHAPTER ELEVEN
# *EXPLORING THE WIDTH*

First came our expanded understanding of the depth; then God revealed the wonders of His heights. Would He also explain more about the width, or breadth as many translations render the Greek word *platos*?[1] At the conclusion of *Volume* 1, Paul wrote:

> I did not have to wait long. In July 2010, while praying for a client, the Lord gave us the first glimpse of the width. I remember it so clearly because I had become very discouraged. Two months earlier our city had sent a letter stating that we had to cease ministry in our location; and now, not only had our efforts to overturn the decision failed, but we had also been unsuccessful in finding a new location. I was determined to have faith for the future, but my emotions would not cooperate with my faith. This day, the Lord revealed that the client was stuck in an ungodly place under a false tabernacle; an unstable location that rotated among the stars so that one could never feel established; a place where doubt and unbelief ruled to such an extent that there would be murmuring and complaining; a place where God would not respond to any need. As we prayed, the Lord instructed us to ask Him to remove the client from this ungodly width. I joined in the prayer for myself, and was totally shocked by what transpired next! Suddenly the doubt and despair lifted off and instantly, I experienced faith. The change was permanent.

> The following weeks would reveal that the width is a place of the heart; a place where faith, hope, and love abide. If past generations have ignored the Lord, or if our lives have not been correctly centered in the Lord, then we have been set up to dwell in the ungodly width, and our hearts have grown weary. To live in the righteous width is to experience the joy of the Father, and we are just

scratching the surface of its complexities.

So what is this scriptural "place of the heart; a place where faith, hope and love abide"? We shouldn't be surprised to find it in what is famously known as the 'love chapter', 1 Corinthians 13:

> *And now abide faith, hope, love, these three; but the greatest of these is love.* [2]

The contrast of Paul's experience in both the ungodly and godly width is also biblical:

> *Hope deferred makes the heart sick, but a desire fulfilled is a tree of life.* [3]

> *A merry heart makes a cheerful countenance, But by sorrow of the heart the spirit is broken.* [4]

Part of our increased understanding of the width initially came together during a time of exploration in which Paul first discerned a tent over the group, which was very limiting. A participant saw us as rotating through the heavens, never being established and never having a home, with a sense of being spiritual nomads in a wilderness. Paul said:

> It is the ungodly tent of meeting, the place of consorting with the enemy. The enemy copies everything. What does this do to us? It limits, instills doubt, clouds the mind; it limits and confuses the gifts. We make ungodly covenants. It's as if we are in a maze but can never get to the end as we keep seeking and never finding. It's a step up from a veil over us; it makes us immobile.

Larry Pearson continued with a prophetic word:

> Going backwards, again; back to the future; the future is behind you. Eternal future, eternal past; wait for the blast. Drilling, drilling, drilling; drilling through the miry clay of your thinking, of your naturalistic unbelief; this is the way it was, this is the way it is; things will never change through soulish unbelief until you come to the solid

foundation of the width of who I am as I AM, and as I am so are you. Drilling through resistance; resistance is futile; drilling through the core to see more of my intention, my redemption. Behold the golden foundation of My width is a living, breathing holy place where you will see my face, for you are my race to run with grace. Could this be the hour where you behold the tower of a holy faith, a heroic faith? (I feel the unwrapping and the re-wrapping of the gift of faith.) I am re-wrapping the package of who you are, and you will be the gift of faith. This will be a North American shift. No longer stay in the outer court of the works; come and become one with the Son behind the veil where nothing is pale, and all is light, and all is one; for the drilling of the Son has begun. Behold, the eyes of the Lord will become clearer before; the eyes of the Lord run to and fro through you. You will see as I see when you learn to be. Run with Me.

Oftentimes, when we receive revelation through discernment, including prophetic words or visions, we must then seek out the scriptural support for it. In this case it takes a bit of digging because the word 'width' in Ephesians 3:18 only occurs in two other verses according to *Strong's Concordance*. *Thayer's Greek Lexicon* reveals that the Ephesians verse means breadth, while Revelation 20:9 implies 'to the ends or corners of the earth' and Revelation 21:16 carries with it the suggestion of great extent.[5] A few verses are nice, but more are better, right? So consider 2 Samuel 22:37, first in the ESV and then in the NKJV:

*You gave a wide place for my steps under me, and my feet did not slip. (ESV)*

*You enlarged my path under me; So my feet did not slip. (NKJV)*

In the Old Testament Hebrew, *rachab* is a verb that means 'to be or grow wide or large', and it occurs 25 times. Psalmists illustrated the blessings of the righteous width:

*I will rejoice and be glad in your steadfast love, because you have seen my affliction; you have known the distress of my soul, and you have not delivered me into the hand of the enemy; you have set my feet in a broad (merchab from rachab) place.*[6]

*I will run in the way of your commandments when you enlarge (rachab) my heart!*[7]

There is plenty of valid proof for the concept of being trapped in an ungodly width that is a maze of hopelessness and confusion versus luxuriating in the righteous width of I AM:

*Therefore Sheol has enlarged (rachab) its appetite and opened its mouth beyond measure, and the nobility of Jerusalem and her multitude will go down, her revelers and he who exults in her.*[8]

*Hear me when I call, O God of my righteousness! You have relieved (rachab) me in my distress; Have mercy on me, and hear my prayer.*[9]

Most of the revelation we receive comes out of both exploration and ministry sessions when a problem is discerned, and then the Holy Spirit leads to breakthrough. During 2013 and 2014, such times led to greater understanding of the width.

In one prayer session, the client was a man whose father had never claimed him as a son, so there had been no bonding and it was as if he had been sabotaged at the very core of his being. His mother, though pleased with his gifts, accepted him only for his accomplishments but never for who he is. Discernment indicated that the result of such un-acceptance by the parents had caused segments of his heart to be trapped in a galaxy in the ungodly width where his creativity had been stolen and he felt depleted; his ability to connect with people was compromised so that he felt used by others, and he could never be content or feel satisfied.

Shortly thereafter, a session with a lady also revealed that parts of her heart were stuck in the stars, in a galaxy in the ungodly width. Her father had never said he loved or was proud of her, and a fractal pattern of separation of fathers from their children was discerned that had begun many generations back.

Another lady complained that she felt like her emotions were not hers, and she had a recurring dream of trying to free people in a prison who were all packed into one cell. It was determined that parts of her heart were trapped in stars within the width of a constellation, the results of which included depression, hopelessness, and mood swings that Paul discerned as dimensional shifting. It was a generational issue of unrest that was shared by her grandmother, which had been empowered by religious self-effort and calling on Mary and the saints for help rather than seeking God. This caused the spirit to be restless because without trust in the Lord there is no peace.

In a similar case, another lady felt as if she was in a barricade and surrounded by 24 wooden pillars. She struggled with confusion in her perception of reality, purpose, and her reason for living. In this situation the root cause appeared to be generational persecution of Christians and confining religious structures, and the barricade or fort was a reflection of this. The day-to-day effect was to stay safe and stay in the familiar, never venturing out into the unknown. There was tremendous sadness because she knew there was more for her but she could not find it. Once again, creativity had been stolen and limits on self -expression had been set in this ungodly width.

On one occasion, Paul discerned part of the 5th eye of the Lord, the spirit of might,[10] in the ungodly width where the connection with a client had been severed. The client had accepted and channeled a spirit guide even though she was a Christian, the terrible consequences of which are illustrated in scripture:

> *Then the serpent said to the woman, "You will not surely die. For God knows that in the day you eat of it your eyes will be opened, and you will be like God, knowing good and evil." So when the woman saw that the tree was good for food, that it was pleasant to the eyes, and a tree desirable to make one wise, she took of its fruit and ate. She also gave to her husband with her, and he ate. Then the eyes of both of them were opened...[11]*

*The lamp of the body is the eye. If therefore your eye is good, your whole body will be full of light. But if your eye is bad, your whole body will be full of darkness. If therefore the light that is in you is darkness, how great is that darkness!* [12]

Paul also noted:

Ezekiel 43:8 appears to say there is a false temple next to the righteous temple:

*When they set their threshold by My threshold, and their doorpost by My doorpost, with a wall between them and Me, they defiled My holy name by the abominations which they committed; therefore I have consumed them in My anger.*

Europa is a goddess meaning 'eyes fully open'. The sin mentioned in this verse created an ungodly place, the first ungodly place created through the eyes. This is the first time humanity agreed with the enemy in a new kind of creation. Just like we can co-create in the kingdom, this was the first effort to co-create with the enemy. Is this the foundation then of all evil kingdoms? It's all about getting secret knowledge or esoteric knowledge. Because we do not trust!

In a final ministry example, Paul discerned a force field trapping spirit parts that was tied to the heart and characterized by despair, dissolution, inability to connect with others, self defense and isolation. As in other instances above, there had been a dysfunctional family in which the client was not valued. In this case, she witnessed her mom's voice being crushed by her dad, an experience validated by the concept in church that women are to be quiet and not speak and not even to think, leading to a sense of worthlessness not only in this lady but also in many women. Paul led her in the following prayer:

Lord Jesus, I understand that as a child I accepted the lie that a female was not to be more than a male would permit. I understand that this has crushed my spirit and caused parts of my spirit to be trapped in the ungodly width. I now reject that lie, and I declare that I will be all that the Lord Jesus has created me to be. Please remove all parts of my spirit that have been trapped in the ungodly width and in the ungodly stars, star systems, constellations and zodiacs. I no longer allow the enemy to project around me that I am worthless and that I am always a victim and powerless. I will take my position in Christ and rule and reign equally with males. Please disconnect me from all fallen sons of God who have perpetuated this lie in my family line.

As they prayed, Paul discerned the fallen sons of God and wrote:

It seems to go back to the sons of God mating with women, where the fallen sons of God were dominant. It was as if the fallen sons of God raped them, owned them, and used them, making a woman's DNA subservient. It put the male in a position of power and seems tied to the pantheon of gods and how the gods treated woman.

Fortunately, our God is so much bigger than the gods:

*The LORD is near to those who have a broken heart, And saves such as have a contrite spirit.[13]*

*He heals the brokenhearted.[14]*

*A merry heart does good, like medicine, But a broken spirit dries the bones. And binds up their wounds.[15]*

Among others, this client's life not only exemplified the hopelessness and depression that exists in the ungodly width, but also led to the understanding that spirit parts get trapped there until such time as faith, hope and love can be restored. Coupling interactive times of ministry or group exploration with scriptures, we have learned much about the width, not the least of which is that when trapped in the ungodly width the mind of man cannot comprehend the mind of Christ, which is accessed in the righteous width of God:

*However, we speak wisdom among those who are mature, yet not the wisdom of this age, nor of the rulers of this age, who are coming to nothing. But we speak the wisdom of God in a mystery, the hidden wisdom which God ordained before the ages for our glory, which none of the rulers of this age knew; for had they known, they would not have crucified the Lord of glory. But as it is written: "Eye has not seen, nor ear heard, Nor have entered into the heart of man The things which God has prepared for those who love Him." But God has revealed them to us through His Spirit. For the Spirit searches all things, yes, the deep things of God. For what man knows the things of a man except the spirit of the man which is in him? Even so no one knows the things of God except the Spirit of God. Now we have received, not the spirit of the world, but the Spirit who is from God, that we might know the things that have been freely given to us by God. These things we also speak, not in words which man's wisdom teaches but which the Holy Spirit teaches, comparing spiritual things with spiritual. But the natural man does not receive the things of the Spirit of God, for they are foolishness to him; nor can he know them, because they are spiritually discerned. But he who is spiritual judges all things, yet he himself is rightly judged by no one. For "who has known the mind of the Lord that he may instruct Him?" But we have the mind of Christ.[16]*

*And do not be conformed to this world, but be transformed by the renewing of your mind, that you may prove what is that good and acceptable and perfect will of God.[17]*

[1] http://biblehub.com/greek/4114.htm

[2] 1 Corinthians 13:13

[3] Proverbs 13:12 ESV

[4] Proverbs 15:13

[5] http://biblehub.com/hebrew/7337.htm

[6] Psalm 31:7-8

[7] Psalm 119:31 ESV

[8] Isaiah 5:14 ESV

[9] Psalm 4:1

[10] Isaiah 11:1-2
[11] Genesis 3:4-7
[12] Matthew 6:22-23
[13] Psalm 34:18 (NKJV)
[14] Psalm 147:3 (NKJV)
[15] Proverbs 17:22 (NKJV)
[16] 1 Corinthians 2:6-16
[17] Romans 12:2

# CHAPTER TWELVE
# *EXPLORING THE LENGTH*

The initial revelation about the length occurred during an intern training in Collingwood, Canada in June 2011. The Lord revealed that the righteous length is a place of unity and oneness, including sexual unity in marriage; it's a place of intimacy. Conversely, the ungodly length is a place where we are incorrectly tied to others, often through pornography or other sexual immorality, and it leads to the place of the dead or the place of the Rephaim:

> *So you will be delivered from the forbidden woman, from the adulteress with her smooth words, who forsakes the companion of her youth and forgets the covenant of her God; for her house sinks down to death, and her paths to the departed (Rephaim); none who go to her come back, nor do they regain the paths of life.*[1]

Going through our collected words and scriptures to write this chapter, I (Barbara) had a sense that time is somehow related to the length because life is literally measured by time segments that are defined as moments, days, and years—length of time, or length of days:

> *I call heaven and earth as witnesses today against you, that I have set before you life and death, blessing and cursing; therefore choose life, that both you and your descendants may live; that you may love the LORD your God, that you may obey His voice, and that you may cling to Him, for He is your life and the length of your days; and that you may dwell in the land which the LORD swore to your fathers, to Abraham, Isaac, and Jacob, to give them.*[2]

> *Wisdom is with aged men, And with length of days, understanding.*[3]

> *He asked life from You, and You gave it to him—Length of days forever and ever.*[4]

> *Length of days is in her right hand, In her left hand riches and honor.*[5]

However, our understanding has been that the length has to do with oneness through sexual union, so what could time have to do with it? But then I came across Jana Green's words from January 2013:

> His breath, the breath of the Almighty; can these bones live? Can they be put in place? Out of line would be out of time; don't make a mistake. Check the dimensions on the place of length where time has invaded. You will take its place. What you are is what you have been; what you are, you already were. Time to align; your inheritance is from above…to align time is from the origin for the knowledge of the holy ones to be restored. Check the place of length, its dimensions to align. You will set by decision to be in right time…

> It is a new day. You have arrived in some ways; you crossed over to a new way of authority to know whom you are and do great exploits. A new day, a new way; I give you permission to explore and to take back what is rightfully yours, What has been lost or given away has been stuck in these places. You have been given everything for godliness. A highway of holiness, a way to Zion; these pathways are in your own heart. From what is old to what is new; it is where you started; it is another level of discernment to know each other for whom you are. For the original design was created good, and the ungodly ones corrupted it by far. The length is the access where deception occurred, for time against time interfered with faith because of what you heard. Faith comes by hearing not just the word. Now, in agreement you discern between the holy and profane. For the knowledge of the Holy One is the Ancient of Days.

I had my ah-ha! God's perfect plans for oneness through sexual unity were derailed in the Garden of Eden. There are varying theories and much speculation regarding what may or may not have actually happened between Satan and Eve, but it is evident that sexual shame entered into the picture simply by the before-and-after verses about Adam and Eve:

> *Therefore a man shall leave his father and mother and be joined to his wife, and they shall become one flesh. And they were both naked, the man and his wife, and were not ashamed.*[6]

> *Then the eyes of both of them were opened, and they knew that they were naked; and they sewed fig leaves together and made themselves coverings. And they heard the sound of the Lord God walking in the garden in the cool of the day, and Adam and his wife hid themselves from the presence of the Lord God among the trees of the garden.*[7]

But how does time play into the scenario? Prior to that first sin, there was no death. God had created Adam and Eve in His image and His intent was that they would live forever, but their eternal life came to an abrupt halt when they chose to eat from the tree of knowledge:

> *Then the Lord God said, "Behold, the man has become like one of Us, to know good and evil. And now, lest he put out his hand and take also of the tree of life, and eat, and live forever"—therefore the Lord God sent him out of the garden of Eden to till the ground from which he was taken.*[8]

Death entered the picture and man's length of days became limited; thus, a definite tie between time and the length. Sadly, when this happened, mankind was plunged into the other ungodly dimensions as well. No longer in the original place of authority (height); faith, hope and love was shattered (width); and mankind was plunged into the death and destruction of the ungodly depth.

Several weeks after this realization, Paul was praying with a man who was concerned about premature death in his family and was surprised when he discerned the ungodly length. Then Paul had his ah-ha as he recalled our conversation about length of days. They began investigating what could have happened since the man's only sexual activity had been with his wife and had never viewed pornography or entered into other sexual sins that would have placed him in the ungodly length. Going further back, it was revealed that a grandparent had exhibited a promiscuous lifestyle and Paul realized that the premature death coming down the generational line was a result of that sin. After prayer to resolve the issue, deliverance was discerned.

> *The Lord is longsuffering and abundant in mercy, forgiving iniquity and transgression; but He by no means clears the guilty, visiting the iniquity of the fathers on the children to the third and fourth generation.*[9]

While dealing with a child in 2013, Paul had the thought that masturbation becomes one with sexual evil; and when abused, the child becomes the recipient of the whole package of generational evil that produces a root of rebellion and becomes a behavioral pattern. Keeping in mind the fact that God often referred to disobedient Israel as an adulteress, or even as a prostitute, Israel's experience illustrates individual experience. While still in the wilderness with Moses, Moab seduced Israel:

> *They invited the people to the sacrifices of their gods, and the people ate and bowed down to their gods. So Israel was joined to Baal of Peor, and the anger of the LORD was aroused against Israel.*[10]

The account of Balak and Balaam in Numbers 22-24 is the key story related to this. In chapter 25, something shifted as the Israelites joined themselves to Baal. Balaam showed Israel how to be willing to enter into the curse:

> *Or do you not know that he who is joined to a harlot is one body with her? For "the two," He says, "shall become one flesh."*[11]

> *For the land is defiled; therefore I visit the punishment of its iniquity upon it, and the land vomits out its inhabitants. You shall therefore keep My statutes and My judgments, and shall not commit any of these abominations, either any of your own nation or any stranger who dwells among you (for all these abominations the men of the land have done, who were before you, and thus the land is defiled),*

*lest the land vomit you out also when you defile it, as it vomited out the nations that were before you.*[12]

Cults always use sexuality, but why? Do fallen sons of God need access to heavenly places? Perhaps they are using us to create in the heavenly places. Do we create places in the dimension during sexual union? It's possible, for we are creative in our nature; and we are created from something, yet created out of nothing:

*By faith we understand that the worlds were framed by the word of God, so that the things which are seen were not made of things which are visible.*[13]

Sexual joining can only happen in a healthy manner between man and wife in marriage; we cannot enter into sexual immorality and expect to receive God's blessings. Fortunately, whether our connection to the ungodly length is via personal or generational sins, thanks to Jesus we can be cleansed and placed into the righteous length of oneness through repentance and prayer.

[1] Proverbs 2:16-19 ESV
[2] Deuteronomy 30:19-20
[3] Job 12:12
[4] Psalm 21:4
[5] Proverbs 3:16
[6] Genesis 2:24-25
[7] Genesis 3:7-8
[8] Genesis 3:22-23
[9] Numbers 14:18
[10] Numbers 25:2–3
[11] 1 Corinthians 6:16
[12] Leviticus 18:25–28
[13] Hebrews 11:3

CHAPTER THIRTEEN

# *CREATIVE ASPECTS IN THE LENGTH*

Recently, as of this writing, revelation has been exploding in terms of identity and the dissociation and dimensional scattering of soul and spirit parts. Most of that is for a future book since God is still in the process of unraveling the threads of a new tapestry of His truth; but Paul's notes from a ministry session in September 2014, hint of much that is yet to be understood and give food for thought regarding the creative aspects of the length. He had discerned that a client was trapped not only in an ungodly length, but also felt him in a door within a new dimension and a couple of sub-dimensions. He wrote:

> Through homosexually the fallen sons of God create in their own image a part; they assign a new identity; they empty the person and make them weak. What is the new identity? The new part is a changed part of the original part, one that has been transformed into something new. It has evolved; it has been distorted; its shape has been changed. How then can it be returned because if it is returned it is forever different? What is the nature of this original part? It is the nascent (undeveloped) sexual part. It causes a rewriting of the sexual DNA code. They have become that!

> What if those who have many sexual partners are constantly creating other identities in the length? Do those other identities affect the person and change them forever? How does the enemy use this for his advantage? He gets to rewrite the sexual code. He wants to create a new humanity, to create a whole new race that will serve him.

> When a husband and wife have sexual intercourse they create a new identity as one, but they also retain their own individual identities. What does this sexual joining between husband and wife have to do with our joining to

the Lord? Ephesians 5:31-32 compares Jesus and the Church to husband and wife. It is a mystery; it is something about the image:

> *"For this reason a man shall leave his father and mother and be joined to his wife, and the two shall become one flesh."* [1] *This is a great mystery, but I speak concerning Christ and the church.*

The key is to operate concurrently in both your new identity and your own identity. It is the same as unity with Christ in which I have a new sense of my identity in Christ but I am still me:

> *Therefore, if anyone is in Christ, he is a new creation; old things have passed away; behold, all things have become new.* [2]

I am new, [3] meaning never I existed this way before. Therefore, in marriage something is created that never existed before. What is the nature of this new identity? Does this new identity then bring us back to the true image of God as male and female? This oneness reflects who God is. What power is there in joining two human beings sexually that was not inherent before? Creativity. The enemy uses ungodly sexuality to create something new for his own purposes.

Paul wondered how the enemy was using the client in this ungodly length and asked the Lord to take them to the Ancient of Days court. It was determined that somehow the original part needed to be unraveled, and what had been created and left needed to be removed. The spirit-tie with the new identity also needed to be severed. The Lord was asked to extract the original client from the hybrid that was created through the ungodly union with sexual abusers, to help him escape the distortion and counterfeit in his life, to restore him to his true self in original design, and to break the ungodly spirit ties with this new creation.

Generally, homosexuality comes down the family line, as is apparent in Romans 1:21-26:

> ...*although they knew God, they did not glorify Him as God, nor were thankful, but became futile in their thoughts, and their foolish hearts were darkened. Professing to be wise, they became fools, and changed the glory of the incorruptible God into an image made like corruptible man—and birds and four-footed animals and creeping things. Therefore God also gave them up to uncleanness, in the lusts of their hearts, to dishonor their bodies among themselves, who exchanged the truth of God for the lie, and worshiped and served the creature rather than the Creator, who is blessed forever. Amen. For this reason God gave them up to vile passions. For even their women exchanged the natural use for what is against nature.*

We've spoken of the width, length, depth and height, but like any physical structure, the separate parts of the human body or of the Church,[4] none stand alone. They are all interconnected, and we'll examine that more as we proceed.

[1] Genesis 2:24

[2] 2 Corinthians 5:17

[3] 1. Vine, W. E., Unger, M. F., & White, W., Jr. (1996). *Vine's Complete Expository Dictionary of Old and New Testament Words*. Nashville, TN: T. Nelson. *kainos* (καινός, 2537) denotes "new," of that which is unaccustomed or unused, not "new" in time, recent, but "new" as to form or quality, of different nature from what is contrasted as old. " 'The new tongues,' kainos, of Mark 16:17 are the 'other tongues,' heteros, of Acts 2:4. These languages, however, were 'new' and 'different,' not in the sense that they had never been heard before, or that they were new to the hearers, for it is plain from v. 8 that this is not the case; they were new languages to the speakers, different from those in which they were accustomed to speak. "The new things that the Gospel brings for present obedience and realization are: a new covenant, Matt. 26:28 in some texts; a new commandment, John 13:34; a new creative act, Gal. 6:15; a new creation, 2 Cor. 5:17; a new man, i.e., a new character of manhood, spiritual and moral, after the pattern of Christ, Eph. 4:24; a new man, i.e., 'the Church which is His (Christ's) body,' Eph. 2:15. "The new things that are to be received and enjoyed hereafter are: a new name, the

believer's, Rev. 2:17; a new name, the Lord's, Rev. 3:12; a new song, Rev. 5:9; a new Heaven and a new Earth, Rev. 21:1; the new Jerusalem, Rev. 3:12; 21:2; 'And He that sitteth on the Throne said, Behold, I make all things new,' Rev. 21:5"* *Kainos* is translated "fresh" in the RV of Matt. 9:17; Mark 2:22 (in the best texts) and Luke 5:38, of wineskins. Cf. *kainotes*, "newness" (below).

2. *neos* (νέος, 3501) signifies "new" in respect of time, that which is recent; it is used of the young, and so translated, especially the comparative degree "younger"; accordingly what is *neos* may be a reproduction of the old in quality or character. *Neos* and *kainos* are sometimes used of the same thing, but there is a difference, as already indicated. Thus the "new man" in Eph. 2:15 (*kainos*) is "new" in differing in character; so in 4:24 (see No. 1); but the "new man" in Col. 3:10 (*neos*) stresses the fact of the believer's "new" experience, recently begun, and still proceeding. "The old man in him … dates as far back as Adam; a new man has been born, who therefore is fitly so called" [i.e., *neos*], Trench, *Syn.* Sec.lx. The "New" Covenant in Heb. 12:24 is "new" (*neos*) compared with the Mosaic, nearly fifteen hundred years before; it is "new" (*kainos*) compared with the Mosaic, which is old in character, ineffective, 8:8, 13; 9:15. The "new" wine of Matt. 9:17; Mark 2:22; Luke 5:37-39, is *neos*, as being of recent production; the "new" wine of the kingdom, Matt. 26:29; Mark 14:25, is *kainos*, since it will be of a different character from that of this world. The rendering "new" (*neos*) is elsewhere used metaphorically in 1 Cor. 5:7, "a new lump." See YOUNG, YOUNGER.

3. *prosphatos* (στερεόω, 4732), originally signifying "freshly slain," acquired the general sense of "new," as applied to flowers, oil, misfortune, etc. It is used in Heb. 10:20 of the "living way" which Christ "dedicated for us … through the veil … His flesh" (which stands for His expiatory death by the offering of His body, v. 10).¶ In the Sept., Num. 6:3; Deut. 32:17; Ps. 81:9; Eccl. 1:9.¶ Cf. the adverb *prosphatos*, "lately, recently," Acts 18:2. *Note:* In Matt. 9:16 and Mark 2:21, KJV, *agnaphos* is translated "new" (RV, "undressed"). Moulton and Milligan give an instance in the papyri of its use in respect of a "new white shirt. See UNDRESSED.

⁴ 1 Corinthians 12

CHAPTER FOURTEEN

# *PUTTING IT ALL TOGETHER*

One passage in the Bible ties the depth, height, width and length all together. It's repeated several times throughout this book not only because it is so relevant but also because it is so powerful:

> *For this reason I bow my knees to the Father of our Lord Jesus Christ, whom the whole family in heaven and earth is named, that He would grant you, according to the riches of His glory, to be strengthened with might through His Spirit in the inner man, that Christ may dwell in your hearts through faith; that you, being rooted and grounded in love, may be able to comprehend with all the saints what is the width and length and depth and height—to know the love of Christ which passes knowledge; that you may be filled with all the fullness of God.[1]*

This beautiful package of hope-filled words from the Lord illuminates the reason this whole discussion is so important. It is in the righteous dimensions of God that we can ultimately begin to understand experientially the vast reaches of His love, which surpass the ability of our finite minds to grasp. Alternatively, when we remain trapped in the ungodly dimensions we endure all of the terrible things our Creator never intended for us to experience.

It is generally understood that the physical creation is a reflection or shadow of the heavenly one, so should we be surprised that God seems to take dimensions quite seriously? Surely we fall very short of understanding His reasons for the oh-so-exact measurements that He dictated to Noah for the Ark[2] or to Moses for the tabernacle and its contents[3], not to mention the specifications for Solomon's[4] and Ezekiel's[5] temples. Additionally, Revelation reveals God's explicit dimensions for the New Jerusalem, a city that is built in the shape of a cube:

> *And he carried me away in the Spirit to a great and high mountain, and showed me the great city, the holy Jerusalem, descending out of heaven from God, having the glory of God. Her light was like a*

*most precious stone, like a jasper stone, clear as crystal. Also she had a great and high wall with twelve gates, and twelve angels at the gates, and names written on them, which are the names of the twelve tribes of the children of Israel: three gates on the east, three gates on the north, three gates on the south, and three gates on the west. Now the wall of the city had twelve foundations, and on them were the names of the twelve apostles of the Lamb. And he who talked with me had a gold reed to measure the city, its gates, and its wall. The city is laid out as a square; its length is as great as its breadth. And he measured the city with the reed: twelve thousand furlongs. Its length, breadth, and height are equal. Then he measured its wall: one hundred and forty-four cubits, according to the measure of a man, that is, of an angel.*[6]

None of these biblical structures can hold together with just one or even two dimensions. Neither do the dimensions we've discussed in this book; and how appropriate that the New Jerusalem is a cube, which also validates our experience!

Years before the Lord began teaching us about the depth, let alone the width, length and height. He introduced the subject of domains[7] to Paul, which he then shared with others who were praying for individuals with dissociative identity disorder (DID). From *Come Up Higher:*[8]

Twelve of us were together one day when the Lord brought to my consciousness what I had learned about these sections of the human body. As I started showing the group what I had learned, revelation began flowing! Somehow, these twelve planes [of the body] are connected to domains. The Lord revealed that there were twelve domains. Each domain has 144,000 cubes.

Looking back, there were as many unanswered questions as there was revelation, but the revelation of domains was indeed the beginning of something much bigger. Before proceeding it is important to remember that the width, length, depth and height are part of God's magnificent creation, just as is everything else that exists:

*For I am persuaded that neither death nor life, nor angels nor principalities nor powers, nor things present nor things to come, nor height nor depth, nor any other created thing, shall be able to separate us from the love of God which is in Christ Jesus our Lord.*[9]

Fast-forward to the present, January 2018, and the Lord is unveiling even more understanding regarding the interconnectivity of His creation. These are things that never would have been imagined more than fifteen years ago when the domains were first realized, and there are still more questions than answers! Undoubtedly, there is much more to come, but this is what we understand now:

- A collection of dimensions is a realm or a domain, and each of the twelve domains, which are made up of 144,000 cubes, is also a whole collection of dimensions
- Width, length, depth, and height are domains or realms; they are places[10] (See also Appendix 1)
- Width, length, depth, and height are also living entities[11]
- Width, length, depth, and height are four quadrants that describe a cube, which looks like one face of a Rubik's cube
- Width, length, and height represent our three physical dimensions, and depth represents the dimension of time
- The enemy has access to certain locations within the dimensions and hides the truth that is there
- DID parts are locked in the various dimensions and in ministry sessions to help set them free, we prefer to pray targeted prayers, which remove the legal rights of the enemy so that he cannot return (as opposed to shotgun prayers that try to hit everything at once)
- Width, length, and height seem to be tied to the stars
- Width, length, depth, and height seem to be a hierarchy; therefore each person has one set

The familiar pattern of a chessboard provides a good visual to enhance our understanding. In Paul's words:

The foundation of the chessboard is the 8x8 grid, and we stand with Melchizedek on a spiritual chessboard. We have been put on the foundation that wisdom has built. It is a cube, in a cube, in a cube. I think it is the Holy of Holies. It is a dimensional grid; it is like multi-dimensional chess. This is a worldwide power system, with the righteous power of God established in the grid. It is the righteous web; it is a power grid.

Remember the phrase, "until you reach the 8", in the discussion of the height? Interestingly, on 8/8/2010, just three months after the original message was received, Larry Pearson delivered a word that included not only height, but also width, length and depth. As you read it, consider the fact that the number 8 in Dreamspeak often means 'new beginnings':

> Greater glory, greater authority, greater unveiling of your apostolic order and era, I'm crossing you over.

> He is overseeing the crossing over into the greater width, length, depth and height, the apostolic order and era that have been initiated from heaven to earth. The government of the Ancient of Days and the unveiling of I AM will unveil the revealed sons of the Most High. The earth will experience what it is to be healed and restored through spheres of authority that will now come under apostolic order.

Clearly, the integration of the righteous realms of all four dimensions is necessary for apostolic order to function according to God's design. On the surface, 'apostolic order' sounds very large scale, so let's downsize the message and make it more personal by looking at a word Jana Green received in August 2016:

> You are establishing from within, aligning to the new creation to begin again. This is the process of restoration that you follow in your inheritance for regeneration; from subcellular to cellular, all will align. What you are seeing is the grid of the heart aligning to the original design; for the

heart itself generates the sound for the soul to agree and the mind to be set free. You are being renewed in your mind from the heart that is humble, for it can be redesigned. And now you are acclimating to what is lovely and pure so connections that are stuck in time will be cured, for eternity was written on your heart. This is the hope of assurance for the regeneration to impart, and it is not that it is new; it was always there, the light, the life and the sound that I truly care. The love you receive is from Me. It is from the heart that is humble because you choose to belief. Now the sound will bring the sight to trust in the hope from the original. Trust Me in this; I will bring you through to the width, the length, the depth and the height made anew. I always have you in the palm of my hand; I never leave you. I am faithful to the heart of man.

That last sentence should be noted, "I am faithful to the heart of man," because as we moved through 2017, hope-filled prophetic words from various contributors continued to be received that tied the condition of man's heart to the dimensions:

Now is the time for the release of the promises of God, for all things that have been hidden are now for you to reveal. His promises are yes and amen, bringing the invisible into the visible, and making it real. To desire to be like him is the best thing you can do; to know him is to love him and trust in His word to be fulfilled. If it hasn't happened yet, it is a worldview of lack; but if it is a promise from the Father that it will happen, this you can bet. Trust is a place of comfort where you are connected by pleasure; it is not something you deserve but rather something you receive, for it is from heaven. Trust in your heart where His throne is set; agree and co-create and claim the best. Look to the beautiful, for it is a plan to prosper; if you see only lack, there is not much to offer… all of the earth is groaning for His image to come forth; creation itself is waiting for the new creation to be born.

Unlock the books, the finished work that you can trust. Under the category of 'abundance' is so much more, and in 'education of the heart', the width, length, depth and height will gather all the parts. It is a plan to prosper and to give hope. You set the path and make the course, and if you lead by His righteousness it will grow brighter for sure. Take off the limits from doubt and unbelief and claim what is truly yours.

Go through; go through to a holy place. Comprehend with all the saints the breath, the height, the length the depth; comprehend all things through Christ who loves to share the fullness of God. Once you step in you will be caught up abundantly above where all things are; through Him who works all things in His glory, you will remove the limits from the power within. With Christ you will comprehend; amen, amen; you must agree not with the impossible but with what you believe...it is laid out before you; your position is sure. Set your heart to your true identity in Christ to rediscover your position in strength and might.

In *Exploring Heavenly Places, Volume 1: Investigating Dimensions of Healing,* We presented biblical evidence suggesting that man's heart, the mirror image of God's heart, exists not only in the body but also in the soul and the spirit.[12] During a coaching session, the Lord revealed that the spirit heart resides in the width, length, and height, and both the soul and physical hearts reside in the depth. How much better off we will be if we understand the aspects of the righteous versus the unrighteous dimensions and learn how to escape the evil versions:

> *...the devil comes and takes away the word out of their hearts, lest they should believe and be saved.*[13]

> *For this reason I bow my knees to the Father of our Lord Jesus Christ, from whom the whole family in heaven and earth is named, that He would grant you, according to the riches of His glory, to be strengthened with might through His Spirit in the inner man, that*

*Christ may dwell in your hearts through faith; that you, being rooted and grounded in love, may be able to comprehend with all the saints what is the width and length and depth and height—to know the love of Christ which passes knowledge; that you may be filled with all the fullness of God.[14]*

It just doesn't get any better than that! In/through our Lord Jesus, we can be set free from the evil places where the enemy seeks to kill and destroy us. Then, in the righteous dimensions of the width, length, depth and height, we can comprehend the majesty and mysteries of God experientially in ways that simply cannot be attained through knowledge. It is all received through faith in Jesus Christ, the only begotten Son of God.

[1] Ephesians 3:14-19

[2] Genesis 6

[3] Exodus 25-28

[4] 2 Chronicles 3-4

[5] Ezekiel 40-43

[6] Revelation 21:10-17

[7] We use the word 'domain' as an expression of what is discerned

[8] Come Up Higher 37

[9] Romans 8:38-39

[10] In *Exploring Heavenly Places, Volume 7: Discernment Encyclopedia for God's Spiritual Creation*, we categorized places as dimensional locations synonymous with domains or realms

[11] In *Exploring Heavenly Places, Volume 7: Discernment Encyclopedia for God's Spiritual Creation*, we categorized as more static than beings, and having a prescribed function. Sometimes they may be manipulated by a being or respond to a command, as when Jesus cursed a fig tree. They may even move or speak, as do elements of creation to declare the glory of God.

[12] Cox, Paul L., Parker, Barbara Kain (2014). *Exploring Heavenly Places, Volume 1: Integrating Dimensions of Healing* (p.38-39). Apple Valley, California

[13] Luke 8:12b

[14] Ephesians 3:14-19

# CHAPTER FIFTEEN
# *LOOKING AHEAD*

It's a pretty safe bet that we've only scratched the surface in terms of understanding the width, length, depth, and height. And, if there's one phrase in the Bible that is the understatement of all understatements, it must surely be the Apostle Paul's words in 1 Corinthians 13:12, *For now we see in a mirror, dimly*—boy, you can say that again! But there is at least one thing we can know now with absolute certainty: when we do see Him face to face our present knowledge and experience of time and space will seem like pre-school because His ways are so much higher than ours[1] that He and His spiritual creation is beyond understanding:

> *Oh, the depth of the riches both of the wisdom and knowledge of God! How unsearchable are His judgments and His ways past finding out! "For who has known the mind of the Lord? Or who has become His counselor?" "Or who has first given to Him, And it shall be repaid to him?" For of Him and through Him and to Him are all things, to whom be glory forever. Amen.*[2]

Think about it. We've seen how length of days, or our lifespan, is tied to time, which is measured by tracking the earth's movement in relation to the sun. But, time as we know it will cease to exist, for there will be no length of days in our eternal future:

> *But I saw no temple in it, for the Lord God Almighty and the Lamb are its temple. The city had no need of the sun or of the moon to shine in it, for the glory of God illuminated it. The Lamb is its light. And the nations of those who are saved shall walk in its light, and the kings of the earth bring their glory and honor into it. Its gates shall not be shut at all by day (there shall be no night there). And they shall bring the glory and the honor of the nations into it. But there shall by no means enter it anything that defiles, or causes an abomination or a lie, but only those who are written in the Lamb's Book of Life.*[3]

Sadly, death, characterized by complete separation from God and Hell with all of it's torments, will still exist for the unbeliever; but that will be out of the realm of consciousness for those of us who have placed our faith in the Lord Jesus. Death will no longer exist for us, nor will any of the terrible afflictions of the unrighteous dimensions. Jesus didn't die for nothing (double negative intended for emphasis!); He died so we can live with God eternally without any of the hindrances, or dimensional fragmentation, that we now endure because of sin:

> Now this I say, brethren, that flesh and blood cannot inherit the kingdom of God; nor does corruption inherit incorruption. Behold, I tell you a mystery: We shall not all sleep, but we shall all be changed— [52] in a moment, in the twinkling of an eye, at the last trumpet. For the trumpet will sound, and the dead will be raised incorruptible, and we shall be changed. For this corruptible must put on incorruption, and this mortal must put on immortality. So when this corruptible has put on incorruption, and this mortal has put on immortality, then shall be brought to pass the saying that is written: "Death is swallowed up in victory."
>
> "O Death, where is your sting? O Hades, where is your victory?"
>
> The sting of death is sin, and the strength of sin is the law. But thanks be to God, who gives us the victory through our Lord Jesus Christ.[4]

It is our fervent hope and prayer that anyone reading this book will choose life everlasting with God rather than the eternal damnation of those who reject His Son, Jesus:

> For God so loved the world, that he gave his only Son, that whoever believes in him should not perish but have eternal life. For God did not send his Son into the world to condemn the world, but in order that the world might be saved through him. Whoever believes in him is not condemned, but whoever does not believe is condemned already, because he has not believed in the name of the only Son of God.[5]

In this life we are a work in progress. As we seek to become conformed to the image of Christ and to put on the mind of Christ,

God is so faithful in His love for us that, even now, He has made it possible for us to escape the unrighteous width, length, depth, and height to a large degree. As we persevere and overcome the trials of life He delivers us from the evil that continually besets us.

> *My brethren, count it all joy when you fall into various trials, knowing that the testing of your faith produces patience. But let patience have its perfect work, that you may be perfect and complete, lacking nothing.*[6]

The generational prayers that God has given us in regard to escaping the ungodly depth and retrieving the treasures of darkness have already been mentioned, but in Appendices 3-6 there are more generational prayers dealing with other aspects of the unrighteous dimensions.

We leave you for now with the priestly blessing of Aaron

> *The Lord bless you and keep you;*
> *The Lord make His face shine upon you,*
> *And be gracious to you;*
> *The Lord lift up His countenance upon you,*
> *And give you peace.*[7]

[1] Isaiah 55:8-9

[2] Romans 11:33-36

[3] Revelation 21:21-27

[4] 1 Corinthians 15:50-56

[5] John 3:16-18 ESV

[6] James 1:2-4

[7] Numbers 6:24-26

## AFTERWARD:
# *LOVE IN THE DEEP*

I (Barbara) was stunned! This book was finished and we were in the process of a final edit before sending it off to the publisher; we even ended with a final goodbye blessing. But then God spoke to my heart this morning. Interestingly, though it always feels wonderful to finish a book, there was something missing this time in my level of satisfaction with the final product. Was I waiting for this and just didn't know it? Perhaps. I guess I'll see when I finish writing it.

I sat down for my morning quiet time with the Lord and began journaling the thoughts of praise in my heart. I'd awakened as I often do with a song playing in my mind, a song I usually consider my song of the day as I begin journaling/conversing/pondering with God. This morning it was just a few words of a familiar old hymn, but for some reason there was no memory of the title or the exact words. My heart sang, "...Jehovah...finding as He promised perfect peace and rest." Only later in an online search did I discover that it was from the refrain of *Like a River Glorious*, written by Francis R. Havergal in 1876:

> Like a river glorious is God's perfect peace,
> Over all victorious, in its bright increase;
> Perfect, yet it floweth fuller every day,
> Perfect, yet it groweth deeper all the way.
>
> *Refrain:*
> Stayed upon Jehovah, hearts are fully blest
> Finding, as He promised, perfect peace and rest.

Now, 146 years later, I pray the impact that Frances' song is still having will be made known to her in the cloud of witnesses. My journal entry:

> Thank you, Lord, for Your peace and Your rest, without which I don't know how I could live.

There is a famous poem that declares, "How do I love thee? Let me count the ways." And that's what comes to mind this morning as I consider how can I praise You with words that are new and fresh. How can I ever adequately express Your magnitude in every aspect of You?

Surprised that I didn't think of this as I wrote the book, I now recalled only one more line of the poem but looked up the whole sonnet to see what else is there:

> How do I love thee? Let me count the ways.
> I love thee to the depth and breadth and height
> My soul can reach, when feeling out of sight
> For the ends of being and ideal grace
> For the ends of being and ideal grace.
> I love thee to the level of every day's
> Most quiet need, by sun and candlelight.
> I love thee freely, as men strive for right.
> I love thee purely, as they turn from praise.
> I love thee with the passion put to use
> In my old griefs, and with my childhood's faith.
> I love thee with a love I seemed to lose
> With my lost saints. I love thee with the breath,
> Smiles, tears, of all my life; and, if God choose,
> I shall but love thee better after death.

How interesting that Elizabeth Barrett Browning began with a biblical expression to illustrate the dimensions of her love for her husband, very much as God's love for us is displayed. Not only that, but she also ended with a reflection of His truth that such love cannot be separated, even by death:

> *For I am persuaded that neither death nor life, nor angels nor principalities nor powers, nor things present nor things to come, nor height nor depth, nor any other created thing, shall be able to separate us from the love of God which is in Christ Jesus our Lord.*[1]

An interesting commentary on the poem is, perhaps, Your message to me today:

> In the first line the speaker expresses her desire to "count the ways" she loves. She only mentions six, a lot for a 14-line poem, sure, but not as many as I expected. The expression of the intensity of her love, therefore, should not be measured in the quantity of expression but in the quality or depth of expression, a depth which equals "the depth and breadth and height / My soul can reach," "to the level of every day's / Most quiet need," and a love that will continue after death.[2]

With that in mind, a simple praise such as, "My Jesus I love Thee," sung from the deep places in my heart says even more than what many individual lines of praise could say, were they lacking the intensity of that deep love? Conversely, one or two simple words directly from Your heart that are spoken directly to the depth of my heart can shake my being and resonate like thunder; for Spirit to spirit communication in the deep cannot be measured.

In the previous chapter, I wrote that "Deep calls to deep" can be about intimacy with God, referring to the deep things of God calling out to the deep things of mankind, a communion of Spirit-to-spirit fellowship. But thanks to His Spirit calling out to me on this morning I know without a doubt that my spirit also calls to Him from the deep places of my heart, and this is all about the love we share. This is the place where we can experience the intensity of God's love and communicate ours for Him in a manner that cannot be put into words.

In the first paragraph I asked, "Was I waiting for this and just didn't know it?" The answer is a definite yes! In fact, the words of Psalm 42:7, "Deep calls to deep," have been attached to a question in my heart for years, "Lord, isn't there more You want me to understand about this?" I knew I was still missing something but today He has answered. As He often does, He sent me on a journey that begins with just a few words and travels through online searches to put together the pieces of a biblical puzzle that showcases His truth.

The Holy Spirit often does something else for me as well: when I write He almost always ties the ending right back to the beginning in some way I could never have thought up myself. Only as I write this do I realize He's done it again! God, my travel agent, has taken me on a journey through His width, length, depth, and height that has taken months, ending it today with one final excursion into the deep places of His heart. And yes, now I am excited about the whole book because now He has completed it.

[1] Romans 8:38-39

[2] http://www.brighthubeducation.com/homework-help-literature/62766-how-do-i-love-thee-analysis/

# APPENDICES 1-7

# APPENDIX 1: ORDER OF KINGDOMS TO DOMAINS

**DOMAINS /**
**REALMS⇔SPHERE⇔GRID⇔GATE⇔CORRIDOR⇔DOOR⇔**
**KINGDOMS**

# APPENDIX 2: QUADRANT CHART

| Height | Length |
|---|---|
| Ruling and Reigning | Oneness Sexual Union |
| Spirit Parts in Stars<br>Star Systems<br>Zodiacs<br>Constellations | Spirit Parts in Stars<br>Star Systems<br>Zodiacs<br>Constellations |
| **Depth** | **Width** |
|  | Heart - Faith - Trust - Love - Hope |
| Soul Parts in Stars<br>Star Systems<br>Zodiacs<br>Constellations | Spirit Parts in Stars<br>Star Systems<br>Zodiacs<br>Constellations |

# APPENDIX 3: NON-EXHAUSTIVE REVIEW OF WHAT IS WHERE?

| Realm/Domain | Unrighteous Aspects | Righteous Aspects |
|---|---|---|
| Width | Unrighteous mind of man | Mind of Christ |
| | Inability to comprehend God | Faith |
| | Fear | Hope |
| | Doubt | Love |
| | Unbelief | Peace |
| | Confusion | Rest |
| | Restlessness | Relationship |
| | Striving | Purpose |
| | Always seeking but never finding | Community with others |
| | Depression | Trust |
| | Hopelessness | Spirit |
| | Mood swings | Spirit Heart |
| | Lack of purpose | |
| | Despair | |
| | Dissolution | |
| | Inability to connect | |
| | Defensiveness | |
| | Isolation | |
| | Worthlessness | |
| | Deception | |
| | Leviathan spirit | |
| | Heart parts | |
| | Spirit Parts | |

| Realm/Domain | Unrighteous Aspects | Righteous Aspects |
|---|---|---|
| Length | Disunity<br>Death<br>Destruction<br>Sexual immorality<br>Spirit parts | Oneness<br>Unity<br>Intimacy<br>Healing<br>Marital sexual union<br>Spirit<br>Spirit Heart |
| Height | Folly or foolishness<br>Control/Jezebel spirit<br>Ungodly powers<br>Spirit parts | Melchizedek<br>Wisdom<br>Powers<br>Forgiveness<br>Ruling and reigning<br>Spirit<br>Spirit Heart |
| Depth/Deep | Infirmity<br>Depression<br>Affliction<br>Grief<br>Fear<br>Torment and torture<br>Desolation<br>Death<br>Stolen and hidden treasures<br>Soul Parts | Treasure<br>Healing<br>Cleansing<br>Sanctuary<br>Restoration<br>God's wondrous works<br>God's mysteries or secret things<br>Intimacy with God<br>Holiness<br>Soul<br>Soul heart<br>Physical heart |

# APPENDIX 4: RULING AND REIGNING WITH CHRIST PRAYER

Lord Jesus, I repent for any decision that I may have made with the enemy before conception because of fear or doubt about your goodness and plan for my life. I understand that this decision may have resulted in the right for the enemy to negatively affect my DNA and RNA and the living water that was to flow out of me. I now exercise my authority in Christ based on the finished work of the cross and the blood of Christ over the contamination of the fiery stones and the living water. I now ask you Lord to remove the influence of wormwood over the living water and purify that water. Lord, please remove me from any ungodly orbs, trapezoids, and geospheres in all dimensions and from the ungodly depth.

Please release into me the fullness of your living water and assign to me all righteous lights. I now ask, Lord, that you will come against all assignments made against me and heal all of my diseases. Please:

- Remove from me any ungodly coating and all ungodly garments
- Remove me from any ungodly constellations and all ungodly zodiacs
- Close all ungodly gates and doors that give the enemy access to me, especially through any ungodly triangles, tetrahedrons, and trapezoids
- Purify all the living water assigned to me
- Remove all ungodly water spirits and seducing spirits

I repent and renounce for all ungodly baptisms and water rituals. Please:

- Remove me from Wormwood and from all ungodly places in the width, length, depth, and height associated with Wormwood
- Disconnect me from all ungodly stars
- Reconnect me according to Your original design to the width,

- Bring all Godly dimensions and quadrants into perfect equality

I repent for all generational bestiality. Please:

- Bring all uncontaminated fiery stones through Your blood back to me
- Remove all animal, fish, bird, and Nephilim DNA and RNA from my DNA and RNA
- Remove all reptilian scales from my eyes and the seven spiritual eyes You have given to me

In the name of Jesus Christ I repent for any time I may have said that I did not want You to make me, that I was angry about how You made me, and I decided that I would remake myself. I repent for any time I was unwilling to yield to You as the clay yields to the potter and for any time I chose the enemy's plan rather than Your plan.

I understand that any decisions I may have made before conception may have given right for the enemy to take the jewels of my spirit into the void and the darkness. I also understand that this may have affected my spiritual authority and my ability to rule and reign, and may have also sealed up the treasures in darkness that you intend me to have.

I acknowledge that in my generational line this may have resulted in phallic worship and the lust of the eyes, declaring that I would produce my own seed without you and that I would save myself through prostitutional idolatry trying to reproduce without You. I acknowledge that my generational line and I may have tried to multiply and fill the earth without You by trying to find secret knowledge. I repent for discontentment with Your ways and Your design of Me. I repent for my discontentment and the discontentment of my family line with how you made me and what you gave to me. I repent for my discontentment and the discontentment of my family line with the authority, position, and place you have assigned me.

I acknowledge that this may have affected the spiritual eyes You have given me and may have resulted in all kinds of barrenness. I ask that You will return through Your blood to me any parts of my spirit that may be scattered in the void. Please resurrect all parts of my spirit. I now declare that I will rule and reign with the scepter that You have given to me. Lord, please correctly align that scepter with the stone in my hand and the seven eyes of the Lamb.

I now repent for trying to be my own sacrifice rather than acknowledging that You are the only sacrifice. I remove myself from the ungodly altar and declare that I am seated with Christ in heavenly places and that I will rule and reign with My God. Lord, please remove any dragons from me that are seated on any thrones.

Lord Jesus, I take my position as a revealed son of God and I stand against the spirit of Shebna who has taken the key of David in my family line and restricted the access that You desire me to have to the house of wisdom and the Godly height and I acknowledge that this spirit has hewn a grave and placed itself in the ungodly height and the ungodly rock, perverting the rock who is Jesus. I now ask that You will throw him away violently, this one who is the leader of the ungodly mighty men. Lord, please seize him and turn violently against him and toss him like a ball into a large country where this spirit will die with all of his ungodly chariots. Please cause him to bring shame to his master's house and drive him out of his office and from his position so that he will be pulled down. I do not allow the spirit of Shebna to cause me to dwell in his ungodly tabernacle.

I now ask that You will take the key of David and place it on Your shoulder, and I declare that You are the rightful authority over the Father's house because the Father has delegated the house to You. I acknowledge that You are clothed with a robe and strengthened with a belt and that all in my household is now Your responsibility.

Lord, I now declare that You are in the role of Eliakim, that You are fastened in a secure place, and that You occupy a glorious throne in Your Father's house. I acknowledge all of the glory of Your Father's house is hung on You and on all Your sons and daughters. I declare that Your glory now fills all the vessels from the smallest to the greatest. Lord, please remove Shebna's peg and the burden that was on it; I cut it off because the Lord has spoken.

I declare that all the gates and doors that Jesus opens will remain open and all the gates and doors that Jesus closes will remain closed. I declare:

- My family and I will no longer be contained by the religious system and by false houses
- My tent pegs will be extended and I will operate in the sphere of authority that the Lord has given to me
- I will no longer be contained by mere men
- I break the power of all those words of containment and all words of jealousy and envy and gossip off of me

Lord, please shut these ungodly gates and doors that encircle me and open up the righteous gates and doors that You are knocking on, giving me the ability to come and go as the Holy Spirit directs.

I break off the power of limitations, of pastors' and leaders' words, and the ungodly words of the body of Christ. I declare that Jesus will be my God and I will be His person, and I choose to submit myself unto others even as they submit themselves unto me. I declare that along with those in the Body of Christ I will now make up the one new man in Christ in which every joint will supply and everyone will do his part.

I am no longer the audience. I am the participant. I ask that You will remove the ungodly rock and declare that the Lord Jesus Christ is my rock and He will destroy the systems of the world and fill the Earth as a great mountain.

# APPENDIX 5: PRAYER TO BE REMOVED FROM THE UNGODLY WIDTH

I repent for my generational line and myself back to before the beginning of time for all of us who did not trust the Lord.

Lord, please break the consequences of all those who were abandoned by parents because of religious activity, and pull my spirit and heart out of any ungodly constellations, zodiacs, stars and star systems. Please remove every part of me from the ungodly width and establish me in the godly width; rightly align my spirit and heart so that I am at peace; stop all dimensional shifting and establish me in peace; and stop repetitive cycles of manic and depressive oscillations. Please remove all ungodly watchers, gatekeepers and doorkeepers on the grid and establish the righteous watchers, gatekeepers and doorkeepers.

I choose to seek after the Lord's wisdom and not after man's wisdom or intellectual understanding. I declare the fear of the Lord is the beginning of wisdom.

# APPENDIX 6: PRAYER TO REJECT DECEPTION ABOUT OUR POSITION IN CHRIST

I reject the lie my ancestors believed, which said that God could not be trusted and we must trust only in our own endeavors and efforts because He did not come through for us.

I repent for my generational line and myself back to before the beginning of time for perpetuating that lie through all successive generations because it was taught and modeled by:

- Each generation claiming they believed but did not practice their supposed faith, thus teaching their children to do the same, and to operate in unbelief

- Not believing that we are more than conquerors

- Having our eyes focused on the earth and its concerns rather than the Lord and His abundant provision in all areas of life, including financial, emotional and spiritual abundance, and physical health

I declare that I will turn my gaze from the things below, set them on things above, and take my seat in heavenly places.

Lord, please focus my gaze upon Jesus, who is the Way, the Truth and the Life. I choose to live my life from above, letting go of the log in the eye of Adam and the generational line, which is the knowledge of good and evil. I choose eternal sight instead of earthly sight. I declare that Christ will live in me and His light will shine out of my eyes.

Lord, please remove me from all places of entrapment and deception in the width, length, depth and height, and from all ungodly heavenly places, realms and kingdoms. I declare I will dwell only in the righteous heavenly places.

# Appendix 7: Prayer of Restitution

Lord, I renounce and repent for those in my family line back to before the beginning of time who broke marriage covenants and mated with the fallen sons of God.

I also renounce and repent for all Moloch and Baal worship in my generational line. On behalf of both sides of the family, please forgive us for choosing to fashion the golden calf at the foot of Mount Sinai when we were too afraid to draw near to You because we feared Your might and power. Forgive us for not waiting for the return of Your servant, Moses, and for breaking covenant with You by worshiping the golden calf through sacrificial burnt and peace offerings.

Forgive us for holding a festival to the golden calf and indulging ourselves in pagan revelry and sexual sin. Most of all Lord, I renounce and repent for first believing, and then declaring, "These are your gods, O Israel, who brought you out of Egypt"; when it was You who set us free from 430 years of Egyptian captivity. Please forgive us for this wanton display of pride, self-deception, stubbornness and unbelief.

Forgive us Father, for not only worshiping the golden calf and sacrificing our children to it, but also for worshiping the star god Rephan, or Saturn, while wandering in the wilderness for 40 years.

On behalf of every ancestor in my family line who entered the land of Canaan after wandering 40 years in the wilderness, I renounce and repent for our refusal to obey Your explicit command not to engage in the pagan sexual practices of incest, adultery, homosexuality and bestiality that were intertwined with the worship of Moloch. Forgive us for sacrificing our sons and daughters in the fires of Moloch in exchange for favor and prosperity. I know this idolatry was a great offense to You, and I now repent and apologize.

On behalf of every ancestor who was involved with Baal or Moloch worship throughout the history of Israel; from the generation who succeeded Joshua, to the reign of Jeroboam, to Ahab and Jezebel, to Manasseh and beyond; I renounce and repent for every evil connected to this false lord-ruler including child sacrifice, sorcery, witchcraft and the worship of the stars of heaven.

Lord, I now ask You to open every bronze door that has been shut in my generational line because of Baal and Moloch worship so that the righteous gates the enemy has closed and contaminated can no longer be shut. Come now King of Glory, flood the heavenly places in my generational line with Your cleansing power and unseal what the enemy has sealed in the heavenly places, making straight every crooked path and smoothing out every rough place. Smash the bronze doors Lord, and sever the iron bars of my captivity. I now declare that what You have opened will remain open and what You have shut will remain shut. Prepare the way of the Lord.

I repent for and renounce all worship of the rulers of darkness in my town, city and state. Please forgive me, my family line and the citizens of this region for worshiping false gods at false altars, sacrificing our children to Moloch, and breaking the covenant of marriage through incest, adultery, homosexuality and bestiality. On behalf of the church, I repent for not fearing Your name, not obeying Your Word, not obeying the leading of Your Spirit; and for presuming upon your grace that we can sin sexually, defy spiritual authority, and not suffer the consequences. Please forgive us for slandering the glorious ones and disconnecting ourselves from Your Glory.

Please disconnect me from the ungodly Mazzaroth and cleanse my spirit, soul and body down to the cellular and sub-cellular levels from all ungodly influence, defilement and power.

Please remove all parts of my triune being from the lowest regions of the ungodly depths by disconnecting me from the Nephilim and Rephaim and removing any witchcraft bands from around my arms.

Please transfer me from Mount Horeb to Mount Zion and reconnect me back to the glorious ones so Your light will shine through me to others as I proclaim the Gospel in power to Jerusalem, Samaria and the ends of the earth.

Please disconnect me from the mountains of Esau and move me to Mt. Zion.

I declare to my spirit that you will be under and submissive to the Holy Spirit; I declare to my body and soul that you will be submissive to my spirit, even as my spirit is submissive to the Holy Spirit.

Lord, please balance correctly the male and female portions of my human spirit.

Please remove all fractal imaging in my family line and remove all mirrors. I declare I will only reflect the image and nature of the Lord Jesus Christ.

Please remove me from the ungodly council and establish me on Mt. Zion and in your heavenly council.

Lord, I repent for those in my family line who turned our family line over to the enemy, thus giving authority for the removal of righteous elders and permission to establish unrighteous elders over us. I acknowledge that these unrighteous elders caused the family to veer off course, moving out of the right time sequence into other time sequences. I now declare, as a revealed son of God, that these unrighteous elders must leave my family line. Father, please establish the righteous elders over my family line and put us back on the right course and into the right time, removing us from Chronos time and placing us into Your Kairos time.

On behalf of the entire church, forgive us for syncing my life according to Chronos time and to my own plans and agendas, instead of Your Kairos time and agenda. Please forgive me for not inquiring of You to see what You want, where You are moving and what You are doing.

Forgive me for believing the lie that Your Second Coming is so close that I need not reach out to the lost and fulfill Your Great Commission. I decree and declare that it is time to align my life with Yours.

Please remove me from Chronos time and sync me with Kairos time. Open every bronze door so that the gates are no longer shut. Open all the righteous doors and flood my life with Your Glory.

Please remove me from any ungodly place in the depth where parts of me are trapped by sonar, and release your righteous sound that will neutralize that ungodly sonar. Please free all of my trapped parts and fragments.

Please break all ungodly ties and connections between myself and the Rephaim or any other person's soul parts, and remove those connectors.

I renounce and repent for those in my family line who traded their souls for favors from the enemy. Please, through the Blood of Jesus, return all scattered soul parts back to my family line and me. I command Beelzebub to leave.

I ask, Lord Jesus, that you will come as the Son of Man and remove all fallen sons of God from my family line and me.

Please disconnect me from Abaddon and remove any parts of me from the bottomless pit.

Please unlock the ciphers and the ungodly algorithms established by the enemy.

I renounce and repent for those in my family line who gave over the family line to the enemy in order to be able to rule and control others for their own advantage and financial gain. I now understand that this gave the enemy the right to cause me to be knit together in the ungodly depth, placing me in a position of servitude rather than one of ruling and reigning over creation, which is my God given right. Please take me back in time to the origin, to your womb of the dawn, and please knit me together in the Godly depth. Please remove from me all DNA and RNA contamination that took place during the ungodly knitting.

I declare that I will not be in subjection to others by means of their control and abuse. Lord, please remove the desolation of generations and take me out of any ungodly places in the depth or the height, disconnecting me from those regions and placing me in the Godly depth and in the Godly height. I reject the discord that has imprisoned me because of my agreement with the ungodly position in which I found myself. I repent for believing the lie that I was to be in submission to others without having any voice, and that this position was normal and was ordained by God.

Please release the righteous sound and vibrations that will align me with the heavenly sounds and vibrations.

Please disconnect me from the dark angels and other unrighteous beings that rule in the ungodly height.

I recognize that my mindset of being a victim has inhibited my ability to fulfill the call on my life to rule and reign under the Lordship of Jesus Christ. I also declare that the wealth that I am to gain for the purposes of the Kingdom of God has been stopped up by my ancestors' sin of wanting personal wealth to use for their own purposes. I now declare that I will receive all the wealth that the Lord wants me to have to fulfill my Kingdom mandate of ruling and reigning. Lord, please release all restrictions against the resources that you originally intended for me to have.

I declare that I will rule and reign in the godly height under the Lordship of Jesus Christ, and I will use all created resources for His Kingdom.

I renounce and repent for my family line and myself for all who entered into sexual activity outside of marriage. Please break the consequences of those who were molested and became victims of sexual abuse. I also repent for all of us who have used pornography for sexual satisfaction. I understand that all this sexual activity resulted in our joining to someone other than our spouses. Lord, as an adult, I ask that You remove me from my parent's sphere of influence and place me in my own sphere of influence. Please remove me from the ungodly length and place me into your Godly length.

Heavenly Father, I come in the name of your Son, Jesus; Your only begotten Son; the only Son of God who became a son of man who takes His place among us, His body. I come into agreement with a common passion to see heaven's intention that was built and established before the foundation of the earth. I ask you, Heavenly Father, Righteous Judge of heaven and earth, to issue a decree against the fallen sons. I call our bloodlines back. Please remove us from the ungodly womb of the dawn. I take back our households in the name of Jesus of Nazareth. I surrender them through the blood of Jesus Christ to be sanctified, glorified, and to come into alignment with their place in the kingdom of Melchizedek. I will no longer drink the wine of the fallen sons of God. I renounce and denounce the spirit of religion, the spirit of debate, the spirit of legalism, the spirit of opinion, the spirit of criticism and the spirit of high-minded intellect. I renounce the mind of the old Adamic way, as well as any mindsets that have been born of the doctrines of the fallen sons of man and the fallen sons of God. I ask for a divorce decree between the fallen sons of God and us. I choose to no longer put faith in the defeated enemy but in the victorious Son of God, Jesus Christ.

Lord, I ask you to reverse the polarity of any ungodly device and extract us from the ungodly collective, removing all microchips, transmitters and receivers. Extract from my mind all voices and communication from others. Remove me from the ungodly width and the ungodly cloud. I choose to no longer to be affected by the ungodly thoughts of others.

Please destroy all molecules, atomic, and sub atomic particles created by the fallen sons of God.

Please destroy any dimensions, kingdoms or spheres that the fallen sons of God created due to the agreement of my ancestors or myself.

On behalf of my family line I repent for all blood that was shed on the land and for all idolatry and sexual sin committed on any land area. Please break all ungodly ties between my ancestors and myself with any land area.

Please remove ungodly words of the fallen sons of God that were added to my original design when I was knit together in the deep.

Please activate any righteous words that were covered up by the fallen sons of God on my scroll when I was knit together in the deep.

Please remove any mismatch and misaligning that took place when I was knit together in the deep; remove all ungodly elders, rulers and powers that were involved when I was knit together in the deep; and remove all stones from the fallen sons of God that were knit into me in the deep.

Please break all ungodly agreements between the ungodly deep and the ungodly height, and disconnect me from all fallen stars, star systems, galaxies, and constellations that were involved in contaminating my original design.

Please remove off of me all contamination from the fallen sons of God that affected the light, sound, frequencies, vibrations and colors that made up my being.

Please remove any genes added by the fallen sons of God. Please repair any genes damaged by the fallen sons of God and return to my DNA any genes that were taken away by the fallen sons of God.

Please destroy any ungodly cloning of my genes and chromosomes. Please undo any ungodly fusion with evil that took place with me.

Lord, I ask that You will come with your measuring rod and linen cord and measure the temple in me, removing all generational ungodly temples, kingdoms, spheres, doors, gates, altars, pillars, priestly garments, worship tools and sacrifices.

[Women] Lord Jesus, I understand that as a child I may have accepted the lie that a female was not to become more than a male would permit. I understand that this may have crushed my spirit and caused parts of my spirit to be trapped in the ungodly width. I now reject that lie and I declare that I will be all that the Lord Jesus has created me to be. Please remove all parts of my spirit that have been trapped in the ungodly width and in the ungodly stars, star systems, constellations and zodiacs. I no longer allow the enemy to project around me that I am worthless and that I am always a victim and powerless. I will take my position in Christ and rule and reign equally with males. Please disconnect me from all fallen sons of God who have perpetuated this lie in my family line.

Father, I recognize that the fallen sons of God did not want to be your sons, and so disconnected themselves from you as Father and established themselves as father. I also acknowledge that this may have resulted in generational parts and parts of me to have been trapped in Saturn, the fallen stars, star systems, ungodly galaxies, constellations and zodiacs and in the ungodly width, length, depth, and height.

I renounce and repent for those in my family line who did the same thing with their fathers, and were so distraught about their fathers that they disconnected themselves from them and declared that they would be fathers without being a child. I understand that this established a disconnection generationally between father and child, resulting in generational blessings not being passed down the family line. I also acknowledge that this may have prohibited me from taking my place as a revealed son of God. I acknowledge that this ungodly fractal patterning may have caused a disconnection between father and child resulting in bitterness and anger in my family line and in my life. I now ask, Lord, that You would remove me from Saturn, the fallen stars, star systems, ungodly galaxies, constellations and zodiacs and in the ungodly width, length, depth, and height.

I now forgive my father and all fathers in my family line for not fathering correctly. I also forgive all sons and daughters in my family line that, because of the cruelty of their fathers, disconnected themselves from their fathers and broke the God-intended linkage between generations, thus also breaking the free flow of generational blessings.

Lord, please connect my generational line and me correctly to the Godly width, length, depth, and height so that I can take my place as a revealed son of God and rule and reign with Christ. I also ask that You will correctly connect me to my generational line so that the generational blessings that were to come down the family line will now be completely restored to the family line and to myself. I reclaim and receive your spiritual blessings that were intended for my family line and me. I now ask that what has happened in the heavenly places will now be done on earth in the physical realm. I now claim all physical, emotional, and spiritual health that you intend me to have. I also claim all physical inheritance that is my right as a revealed son of God.

Lord Jesus, by your life sacrificed on the cross and by your life-blood, please dismantle and remove all structures that have been built from these sins and from unclean spirits, including ungodly habits, curses, devices, conduits, attachments, lies, 'gifts' or deposits. Free us from ungodly structures, from distortions in my life and family line, and even from any distortions of our DNA and RNA. God Almighty, please close any doors or openings that these sins and ungodly structures created. Open any godly doors to you and your blessings that these sins and ungodly structures had closed. Holy Spirit, please empower righteous choices in my family line and myself. I choose to honor You, growing godly habits while enthroning Your name in our lives, relationships, and land.